Shultz
Bakelite Jewelry

MW00563281

Karima Parry

Schiffer Publishing Ltd®

4880 Lower Valley Road, Atglen, PA 19310 USA

Copyright © 2002 by Karima Parry
Library of Congress Control Number: 2002108802

All rights reserved. No part of this work may be reproduced or used in any form or by any means—
graphic, electronic, or mechanical, including photocopying or information storage and retrieval
systems—without written permission from the copyright holder.
"Schiffer," "Schiffer Publishing Ltd. & Design," and the "Design of pen and ink well" are registered
trademarks of Schiffer Publishing Ltd.

Designed by Bonnie M. Hensley
Cover design by Bruce M. Waters
Type set in Mona Lisa Solid/Korinna BT

ISBN: 0-7643-1662-1
Printed in China
1 2 3 4

Published by Schiffer Publishing Ltd.
4880 Lower Valley Road
Atglen, PA 19310
Phone: (610) 593-1777; Fax: (610) 593-2002
E-mail: Schifferbk@aol.com
Please visit our web site catalog at **www.schifferbooks.com**
We are always looking for people to write books on new and related subjects.
If you have an idea for a book please contact us at the above address.

This book may be purchased from the publisher.
Include $3.95 for shipping. Please try your bookstore first. You may write for a free catalog.

In Europe, Schiffer books are distributed by
Bushwood Books
6 Marksbury Ave.
Kew Gardens
Surrey TW9 4JF England
Phone: 44 (0) 20 8392-8585; Fax: 44 (0) 20 8392-9876
E-mail: Bushwd@aol.com
Free postage in the U.K., Europe; air mail at cost.

Dedication

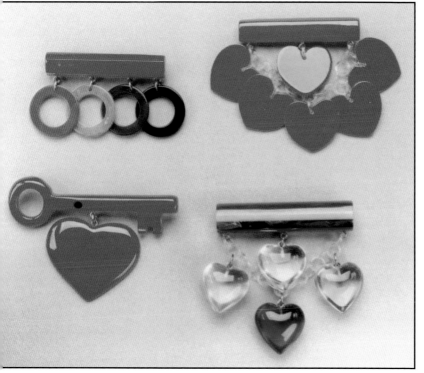

For my adored husband, Aziz, who has superb patina. The first time he watched me slide on six Shultz bangles per arm while dressing to go to a fancy party with him, his comment was "Those look great!" The second time while watching me selecting Shultzes to wear to another party, he suggested a different combination than the one I had originally chosen. He was right. They looked even better than the ones I had picked. May God give us many years of loving oxidation together.

When all is said and done, it's all about loving and being loved. For those people both here and gone whose love has warmed my life.

Acknowledgments

My heartfelt thanks to Ellen Poss and those collectors both acknowledged and anonymous whose Shultzes appear in this book. Thank you for sharing your treasures. My editor, Douglas Congdon-Martin, combines patience with a wonderful eye, and I thank him for being a pleasure to work with as always, and for making this book beautiful. Special thanks to the photography staff at Schiffer Publishing. Of course, this book would never have been possible without the kind help and cooperation of Ron and Ester Shultz. In addition to being patient with my endless questions and queries, they helped me to get in touch with Shultz collectors far and wide to track down their pieces so that they could appear in this book. This book was a labor of my love and respect for Ron and Ester Shultz, and for their glorious magical Bakelite.

Contents

A Brief Introduction to Bakelite

Two one-of-a-kind Bakelite signs by Shultz, with all hand carved letters. The larger one measures 18" long. $900-1000, each. Barbara Wood.

Bakelite, a phenolic thermoset plastic, was concocted by Leo Baekland in the late 1920s. It was among the first of the man-made plastics. Bakelite in its original formulas, which included phenols and formaldehyde, has not been produced for almost 50 years. Along with use in electrical components, household objects and other industrial and semi-industrial applications, Bakelite was quickly discovered by costume jewelry manufacturers of the day. Spurred on by the market constraints of the Depression, and attracted by its endless range of colors and transparencies, its availability, low price, and the ease with which it could be worked, Bakelite became the material of choice for inexpensive costume jewelry in the 1930s. The war years and war demand for metal, which made it scarce for use in costume jewelry, just served to strengthen Bakelite's appeal for use in costume jewelry through the 1940s.

But by the 1950s costume jewelry manufacturers again had abundant supplies of metal and large scale importation of rhinestones from Europe added a sparkly new palette of colors that complemented 1950s fashion trends. While most Bakelite jewelry required hands-on manufacture to carve and decorate, many kinds of metal costume jewelry were better suited to mass production techniques. However, in spite of the impact of these developments, it was arguably the advent and growth in use of Lucite, another plastic material that was developed by the DuPont Corporation, which brought the Bakelite era to a close. Lucite did everything that Bakelite could and was less toxic to manufacture and work with.

In terms of the work of Ron and Ester Shultz, what matters most about the fact that they have chosen to work primarily in Bakelite is not how Bakelite was invented, by whom, what it is made of, or when or where it was made. That Ron and Ester Shultz, who are in essence modern artists, have chosen to express themselves creatively utilizing a material that can be up to 75 years old, and has not been manufactured in its original recipes for almost half a century sets their work apart from other modern artists who work in plastics. Not only is their work of value as art, but the materials that they work with have an intrinsic value of their own.

Some colors of Bakelite (like purples and aquas) and some kinds of Bakelite (such as Stardust, which was manufactured for only one year, 1936-37) are rarer than others, and the value and desirability of certain Shultz pieces that include these rarer materials is enhanced. In addition, although Ron and Ester Shultz work almost exclusively in Bakelite, a few of their earlier pieces were made in Lucite. Because these early Shultz pieces in Lucite are significantly less common than those made of Bakelite they have a special cachet. However, as Bakelite disappears into collections and the availability of raw material is an increasing problem for the Shultzes, it is possible that in the future they may make more pieces utilizing Lucite, which is a much more readily available material.

Bakelite as a material has a few unique characteristics which make it behave almost as a "living" medium. Chemically, the material can sometimes be unstable, depending on what fillers were used at the time of manufacture. The effects of this can be seen in the degradation of the surface area of some of the colors that can occur over time. This property is known as oxidation. The effects of oxidation "age" Bakelite, changing its color, transparency, and lustre, and can radically transform its appearance. Some colors tend to degrade more quickly than others. In newly made pieces of Shultz the effects of oxidation are not readily apparent as final polishing brings the material back to its glowing glorious original colors. I like to refer to these colors as the "Primary Palette." However, over the years, the effects of oxygen and exposure to light, especially sunlight, upon Bakelite can be dramatic. All Bakelite, including Shultz pieces, is affected to some extent by oxidation. Oxidized Bakelite colors could be called the "Secondary Palette."

Since the Shultzes have been working in Bakelite for less than 20 years, it will take more time for their pieces to show profound effects of oxidation. But some of their earliest pieces, especially those made of white Bakelite, are now starting to show pronounced effects of oxidation. White Bakelite turns increasingly ivory over time, sometimes taking on a golden hue. Another place to observe the effects of oxidation are in the darkening that begins to appear at the edges of polka dots where the material is quite thin and oxidizes more rapidly than the center of the dots where the material is thicker. This is also true of the thinnest edges of carved areas.

In terms of how their designs utilize color, the Shultzes are well aware that their Bakelite palette of colors are a living medium, and that oxidation will transform the appearance of their pieces over time. Not only do they consider how the colors they choose will work when they first create a piece, but they and the collectors who buy their pieces also anticipate how the colors will change, and what the piece will look like as it ages. This can lend an element of unpredictability to Shultz Bakelite pieces. A few years after collectors pay a special premium to have pieces that include a few valuable slivers of the rarest colors of Bakelite such as pinks, purples, or aquas, those colors will disappear behind a veil of oxidation. Pink-toned Bakelite will gradually mutate into coral tinged orange tones, and the especially coveted lavenders and purples will slowly brown. The change is only skin deep, and diligent repolishing with Simichrome can restore the colors back to their original hues. But Bakelite is by its very nature and composition an unstable material, and the magnificent pinks and purples can only be captured briefly. They are especially precious because they are fleeting as well as rare.

My First Shultz Bangle

I remember when I acquired my first piece of Shultz Bakelite. I had seen a few of their pieces in a friend's collection, and through her I was able to contact them. They no longer do pieces to order for customers, but in those days they did. So, I sent them a large square vintage Bakelite bangle that was a deep Creamed Corn color and asked them to cover it with small, multicolored polka dots.

When the bangle arrived back from the Shultzes and I unwrapped it, I almost had a heart attack! To someone who was completely unaccustomed to the primary Bakelite color palette, the colors of the polka dots were too bright, too loud, too intense, and the creamed corn bangle was now pure snow white, a color simply unheard of in vintage Bakelite.

It didn't go with any of my vintage bangles, and it took an act of Bakelite fashion courage to slide it on my wrist and leave the house. But when I finally mustered up the moxie to wear it, people's reactions to it were surprisingly enthusiastic. Everywhere I went, total strangers grabbed my arm and wanted to see it more closely. Many people asked where I got it, and where they could get one like it. People who couldn't care less about Bakelite, or plastic jewelry for that matter, went wild over it. And almost everyone who saw it started to laugh! This bright happy bangle made friends wherever it went.

Vintage Bakelite collectors and dealer friends praised it gingerly. They could not help recognizing the great craftsmanship, but they too found the colors gaudy and jarring, and because it was white some of them were unconvinced that it was Bakelite at all. The more I wore it, the more I got used to the colors and the happy appearance of this bangle, and pretty soon it occurred to me that it would be nice to have another Shultz bangle to wear with it.

That was the beginning of my own infatuation with Shultz Bakelite. Over the years, although I have not surrendered my devotion to vintage Bakelite, I have amassed a serious collection of Shultz bangles — many of which appear later in this book. My infatuation has deepened into an enduring affection and appreciation for Shultz pieces. They are carefully designed and meticulously crafted, and they are modern art in their own right. They deserve their place as the Bakelite collectibles of the future.

My prototype square dotted Shultz bangle is now a few years older than it was when it appeared in my first book, *Bakelite Bangles Price and Identification Guide*, on page 125. It is no longer pure white. It has oxidized to a rich cream color, and the Shultzes have told me that many people have asked for one just like it.

Above: In this photo, taken when the bangle was almost four years old, it is clear that the bangle is slowly reoxidizing back to cream. A chunky Bakelite rounded square, with multicolored confetti dots. 1" wide, 3/8" walls. $450-550. Karima Parry.

Ron and Ester Shultz

Ron and Ester Shultz.

Ron and Ester Shultz make their home in Lakeland, Florida. Ron was born and raised in Somerset, Pennsylvania. When I asked what sort of work he did before discovering Bakelite, Ron replied, "I have had many jobs including farm work, medic, factory work, truck driver, lawn moving service, etc. I hated milking cows but did a good job on the factory lines. I was mostly always ahead of everyone else. I was a truck driver when I met and married Ester. She is from Florida and was raised in Bradenton. Soon after we married we went into business for ourselves and had a lawn mowing service for a couple of years. We discovered the flea market business and started collecting things so we could do that on the weekends and enjoyed it so much we gave up the lawn mowing business and turned to antiques."

Ron and Ester's work has evolved over the last decade from rather modest beginnings. Ron explained: "We have been making Bakelite jewelry for about 10 years now. When we first started making jewelry all we had for tools was a hack saw, a piece of sand paper, some furniture polish and a piece of leather. I would cut the pieces with the saw, sand the edges with the paper and buff and polish with the leather. It was primitive, but for what we were doing at the time it worked!"

In the early years, one of the first people who helped Ron and Ester get started by supplying Bakelite for them to work with was their dear friend Chuck Piantiere. Over the years, Chuck has continued to supply them with pounds and pounds of Bakelite, and Ron and Ester say that they could never have made many of the wonderful carved pins if Chuck had not been there to help them to find appropriate material.

When asked if they considered themselves to be artists, Ron commented, "I guess we are artists because God has shown us how to do what we do. He has shown me every step of the way and has taught me things that I would have never figured out on my own. After 10 years it is much easier now. It was very hard at first."

One thing that sets the Shultzes apart from other modern artists who make jewelry is their choice of Bakelite as their medium. "We chose to work with Bakelite because it was more valuable and more beautiful than other things. The colors are wonderful. The material is easy to carve and when it is finished it is awesome." However, the Shultzes' choice of an antique material has obliged them to tap unconventional sources to find enough material for their art. "We have used many things to cut and make pins out of, from poker chip holders to Mah Jong trays, trophy bases, dice, chips, you name it we have used it. The hardest to cut up are the radios that are black or brown. Those are made of a special formula that is harder and the blades do not want to cut it. So we steer away from using these pieces."

Although quite a bit of Bakelite was produced from the 1920s to the 1950s, certain colors were made in greater quantity than others, and some colors are downright rare. "We find the rarest colors are purples and pinks, black and Applejuice." The color term Applejuice can be confusing. It refers to transparent golden yellow Bakelite. However there are actually two colors of Bakelite that are Applejuice. The first is the material that was transparent yellow when it was manufactured. The second was transparent and colorless when manufactured, but has yellowed as it oxidized and turned into Applejuice. After a few years, these colors are indistinguishable from one another, and collectors refer to both as Applejuice.

Other colors were produced in large quantities. Ron noted that "The more common colors are red, yellow, green, maroon and white or what today is called Butterscotch. It is called Butterscotch because the oxidation has changed the color from white to Butterscotch." Actually, most vintage Bakelite collectors know the color Ron is referring to as Creamed Corn. This material was white when first manufactured and ages to an increasingly creamy hue. The color that vintage Bakelite collectors refer to as Butterscotch actually was originally a deep yellow that acquires deeper golden overtones as it oxidizes, and it is somewhat rare.

In other words, when discussing Bakelite color nomenclature can be confusing. There are actually two basic color groups to consider. The first is the primary Bakelite palette, which is the original colors as they were when manufactured. This astonishing range of colors is revealed when the oxidation is polished away. The Shultzes are intimately familiar with these colors. The secondary Bakelite palette is that same range of colors as they appear after a number of years of exposure to light and air and are showing the effects of oxidation, which include browning, yellowing, graying, etc. This is the Bakelite palette that is familiar to vintage Bakelite collectors. In general, the primary palette of colors was bright, vibrant, rich, and intense. The secondary palette of colors is mellow and aged, and in many instances they have little resemblance to primary Bakelite colors.

As an artist, Ron Shultz has a special challenge working with colors. He confided, "I have trouble with some of the colors because I am color blind to some extent. I have a problem distinguishing between browns and red and some blues and purples. Most of the other colors I can see and the Lord helps me to get them right."

This may explain some of the unconventional color combinations that occasionally appear in Shultz pieces. When I first started collecting Shultz Bakelite, I did notice that the occasional piece inexplicably included a single oddly colored dot or checker that didn't quite blend in with the others in the design. I attributed it to scarcity of material, and the possibility that they ran out of the required color during fabrication. However, another explanation that had occurred to me was that the Shultzes, like many of the devoutly religious patchwork quilt makers in 18th and 19th century America, believed that no one could make anything perfect except God. So, they deliberately included little quirky imperfections out of respect for God and their faith. The true explanation may simply be that sometimes Ron doesn't notice the occasional dot or checker which gets worked into a piece that happens to be a slightly different color than all the others in the design.

Working with a material that hasn't been manufactured in roughly half a century means that Ron and Ester have to be frugal with it. Ron disclosed, "I save every scrap of Bakelite. I never throw anything away because I can go back two years from now and find a piece that just fits where I need it or will give me an idea of something else to make."

But some of the patterns they make are more wasteful of material than others. Ron notes that, "The checkerboards and the Belle Kogan style dots — especially the double BK's are very costly material-wise."

One of the most engaging characteristics of Shultz Bakelite is that although many of the pieces clearly are inspired by vintage designs, the Shultzes reinterpret these designs and manage to come up with pieces that are a charming synthesis of old and new. A Scottie dog pin, for example, which is one of the classic Bakelite pin motifs, is Shultzified when the Scottie appears wearing a hat and smoking a pipe, or armed with a fishing rod. Shultz Scottie pins have attitude!

Ron and Ester say that they are "... not into the fashion trends. Bakelite seems to always be a trend of its own. We hunt for patterns everywhere we go and in everything we see. Greeting cards, fabrics, books, things the grandkids bring home from school. Our flamingo pin is taken from our shower curtain. We enjoy making things from both eras, both today's designs and yesterday's. In Bakelite they blend so well together."

The Shultzes have made all kinds of things in Bakelite, including a few tabletop sculptures, and some of their pins are so large that it is unlikely that they could be worn very often, if at all. But the bulk of their work is in two forms: pins and bangle bracelets. Pins are arguably the form where Ron and Ester have the most freedom to express their design ideas. Whereas bracelets, especially bangles, must be round, and of a certain size, etc., pins have no such constraints. Pins can be tiny or huge, and of every conceivable shape.

A very rare older bracelet composed of masses of Bakelite buttons attached to a celluloid chain. Ron and Ester Shultz.

A straw hat, trimmed with Bakelite buttons. This may be a one-of-a-kind. Ron and Ester Shultz.

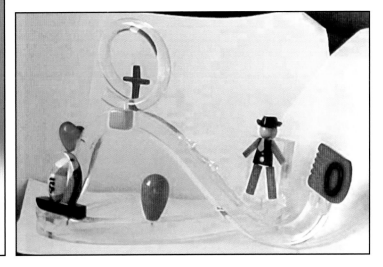

A one-of-a-kind Bakelite ship tabletop piece. Ron and Ester Shultz.

A one-of-a-kind Bakelite sailboat tabletop piece. Ron and Ester Shultz..

This is what Ron and Ester call a "Compulsive Art Piece." Made of Lucite and Bakelite. 18" long. $900+. Barbara Wood.

This is a one-of-a-kind Bakelite art piece. It is huge and surprisingly heavy. Measures 12" tall x 8" across and the material is 1/2" thick. $3,000. Barbara Wood.

Ester does all the reverse carving. She says that she has improved over the years because she has "...learned to pay more attention to detail and not worry so much about the brace-let itself." The fact is that transparent blank vintage Bakelite bangles that are suitable for reverse carving have become scarcer and more costly as the years have passed. The Shultzes acquire them when they can find them, but they are mindful that a mistake can be expensive, and a serious mistake can spell disaster. She comments, "You can worry about messing up an Applejuice bracelet blank that cost lots of money or just go ahead and enjoy doing the work and it usually comes out better."

Ester Shultz.

Ron and Ester Shultz are a team, but each of them specializes in various kinds of pieces or techniques. For example, Ron prefers making bangles. "I find the easiest for me to do is the bracelets. The designs seem to be endless and if there is one that I am not happy with or mess up, I throw it in the bucket and a year or so later go back and fix it or by then know how to improve it. For me the hardest or most labor-intensive are the confetti bracelets. They are very time consuming."

Ester finds the painting the hardest thing for her to do. She says that "All of the work has its own degree of difficulty and it is hard to say which is easiest or which is the hardest to do. It is all very time consuming and has to go through various steps from start to finish to make a piece of Bakelite into the beautiful new piece you see when it is finished."

As Ester's expertise in reverse carving has evolved, so has Ron's technique for making their famous checkerboard bangles. "At first the checks were hard and confusing to make but I knew if I worked at them they would eventually come around and they did. Thank God. The first ones looked like a big mess before they were finished which made me work faster and harder until each piece was finished." Some of the earliest Shultz checkerboard bangles include "compensation pieces." These are small pieces of Bakelite that were worked into the almost finished bracelet when the piece was nearing completion and the pattern did not quite line up precisely at the end. The presence of "compensation pieces" is one way to distinguish an earlier Shultz checkerboard from a more recent one. In the last few years, Ron has mastered the art of making astonishingly precise checkerboard bangles, which don't require "compensation pieces" anymore.

Ron Shultz.

A very early red, yellow, green, and black Bakelite checkerboard derivative bangle, bordered with custard marble, constructed over a creamed corn liner bangle that has an interesting inlaid green triangle. 1-3/4" wide, 3/8" walls. $850-1100. Helene Lyons.

Shultz Bakelite is addictive, and few collectors can stop at owning just one piece. However, during the two decades that the Shultzes have been making Bakelite jewelry, I wondered if collector's tastes had changed much. Ester replied, "We have not had any problems with collector's taste changing much. They have been concentrating on the bracelets the last few years but we have also been making and selling pins as we go along. And we are noticing an increase in that volume also. At first collectors were more interested in the reds and blacks and greens and yellows — what we call the Philly colors. But since they have seen how beautiful the original colors are under the oxidation some of them have switched to preferring the pastels. It is all a matter of taste."

The "Philly" colors that Ester refers to are the classic range of colors that are used on a particular pattern of vintage hinged Bakelite bangle. This bracelet incorporates a pair of spectrums of geometric fins that are laminated together and then set facing each other across the top of a hinged bracelet. This singular style of bracelet became known as the "Philadelphia" bracelet when a bidding war developed between two well known Bakelite collectors over one of these bracelets that was offered for sale at an antiques show in Philadelphia some years ago. The piece was fought over until the price rose to a level that was previously unheard of for a piece of Bakelite jewelry. Hence, the Bakelite collecting world was changed forever, and the whole episode was immortalized with the naming of the bracelet in honor of the venue where the incident took place.

I asked Ron if Ester has held on to any of their work. Ron revealed that "...There are only a few pieces in our collection and they are things that I have made for Ester personally. I made a red cross for her that has the name Jesus inlaid across

This is an older one-of-a-kind Shultz rendition of the famous Philadelphia bracelet. Red, green, yellow, and black Bakelite fins on top of a black Bakelite clamper bangle. $1500. Helen Zeve.

it that was from our sterling wedding bands. She likes to wear it to church. And I made a bracelet that has crosses and stained glass windows inlaid in it. She also has the first checker bracelet that I made. I believe there is a little Scottie that she keeps that she likes a lot also."

Through the years that I have gotten to know Ester and Ron Shultz, I have discovered that perhaps the most remarkable thing of all about them is not their jewelry. Instead, it is their total commitment to their faith and the work of their church. This is what Ron and Ester Shultz care most about, and a significant portion of the proceeds from the Bakelite jewelry that they make and sell goes to support their church, and its many activities and programs to help those who are less fortunate than they have been. They are deeply believing and have dedicated themselves and their lives to helping others.

A group of three early cherry red Bakelite cross pins. There were not many of these made. Small: 2" x 1-3/8" $80-100. Medium: 3" x 1-7/8" $90-120. The largest one has the same overall dimensions as the medium, but it is made from wider pieces. $100-130. Helene Lyons.

They told me, "We are very much involved here with our church and spend a lot of our time on call for the church to go and pick up food for our community center where we give bags of groceries to needy families in Lakeland. We work around this schedule because this is one of the most important things in our lives. We know that this is what we were called to do and that God gave us the jewelry business so that we could be available to do His work. We can be making a bracelet and get a call and we will put it aside and come back to it when we are finished with what He wants us to do. There was no one but God to teach us how to do what we do. Without Him we could do nothing."

Shultz Bakelite collectors can take special pride in wearing their pieces because each piece that leaves the Shultzes' hands has helped put food on the tables of people who need it or helped to finance other acts of charity. Ron commented, "He has put it on the hearts of many people to buy our things and help provide us with the material that we need to keep this going. To Him and to those many people we are eternally grateful. You will never know this side of Heaven how you are helping so many people." Ron and Ester are grateful to the collectors who have supported them and enabled them to help others. They asked me to "...Send you all our thanks and blessings in the name of Jesus."

Understanding Shultz Bakelite Jewelry

Before plunging into Shultz Bakelite jewelry, there are a few aspects of it that the reader should understand. To begin with, Shultz pieces are all made by hand, one at a time, from material that can be scarce and difficult to find in uniform colors and in quantity. Although some designs, such are checkerboard bangles, are made repeatedly, a close examination of two seemingly identical pieces will almost always reveal that there are subtle differences between them. Exactly identical Shultz pieces are very rare indeed. In two seemingly identical checkerboard bangles, for example, sometimes the checkers are not quite the same exact size on both bangles, or there is a subtle difference in the proportions of each of the bangles.

There are also subtle differences in the sizes of the checkers between these seemingly matched pair of green and blue Bakelite two-row checkerboard bangles. 1" wide, 3/8" walls $1000-1200 each. Private Collection.

When examining this seemingly matched pair of red and camphor Bakelite two-row checkerboard bangles, note that there are minute differences in the sizes of the checkers, and other subtle details which confirm that it is almost impossible to make absolutely identical pieces. 1" wide , 3/8" walls. $1000-1200 each. Barbara Wood.

On the bottom, an overscaled iris blue and transparent Bakelite two-row checkerboard bangle. 1-1/4" wide, 1/2"+ walls. $1300. On the top, a newer, smaller scaled daffodil and applejuice Bakelite two-row checkerboard bangle. 7/8" wide, 3/8" walls. $900. It is only by viewing these together that the stark differences that can exist in the proportions of two-row checkerboard bangles become very obvious. Barbara Wood.

Because of the availability of material, sometimes the checkers on each bangle might not be exactly the color or degree of marbling. This is well illustrated by this identical-at-first-glance pair of black and transparent green two-row checkerboard bangles. Note that the transparent green in the bangle on the right is a slightly darker and a more bluish hue than the material used in the bangle on the left.

On this pair of multicolored transparent two-row Bakelite checkerboard bangles, although they both have the same colors of material, in roughly the same amounts, the layout of each bangle is totally different. The bangle on the left is done in a random layout, while the bangle on the right is carefully laid out in a precise diagonal pattern. Although they are complementary, they are hardly an identical pair.

A matched pair of two-row Bakelite checkerboard bangles. These are interesting to view together because, on first look, they appear to be an exact match, whereas in the lower bracelet the transparent green squares are actually all the same uniform color, while in the upper bracelet, the transparent green squares are subtly different shades of green, including a number of squares that are distinctly bluish. 7/8" wide, 3/8" walls, each. $750-800 each. Lower bangle Helene Lyons, upper bangle Karima Parry.

A pair of multicolored all transparent Bakelite two-row checkerboard bangles. One has a symmetrical layout, the other has a random one. 7/8" wide, 3/8" walls, each. $800-875 each. Karima Parry.

Sometimes because of the way the colors are combined, a pair of pieces is actually not a pair at all. For example, on this pair of multi colored checkerboard hat pins, although they initially appear to be a matched pair, the amounts of blue and red checkers in each pin are not the same. The hat on the right has more "blue" while the hat on the left has more "red." It gives each of them a distinctly different look.

The proportions of colors in each piece can also drastically alter the appearance of a piece. These two-row checkerboard bangles are both made of red, yellow, and black Bakelite. Both bangles are constructed in a diagonal pattern. However, the bangle on the left has a much lower proportion of black than the bangle on the right, producing a much lighter, livelier looking bangle. The bangle on the right appears darker, more formal, and a little more sedate.

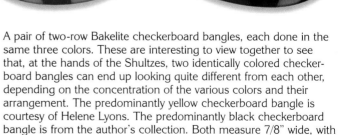

A pair of two-row Bakelite checkerboard bangles, each done in the same three colors. These are interesting to view together to see that, at the hands of the Shultzes, two identically colored checkerboard bangles can end up looking quite different from each other, depending on the concentration of the various colors and their arrangement. The predominantly yellow checkerboard bangle is courtesy of Helene Lyons. The predominantly black checkerboard bangle is from the author's collection. Both measure 7/8" wide, with 3/8" walls. $750-800 each.

A pair of multicolored opaque Bakelite checkerboard hat pins, with Scottie dog dangles. 2-1/2" across. $500, each. Private Collection.

The Shultzes often repeat a design but with slight variations. Note that there are many differences between these two cat and fishbowl pins. Each cat's eyes are done in a different technique. The cat on the left only has one fish in her bowl, but the cat on the right has two fish to chase. The difference between these two pelican pins on the next page is more dramatic. Although they are the same pattern, because the Shultzes did each of them in totally different colors of Bakelite they are quite distinctly different from each other.

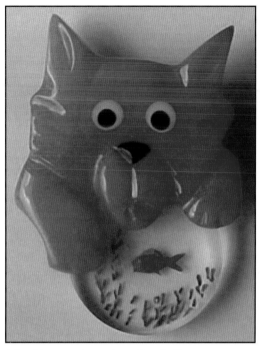

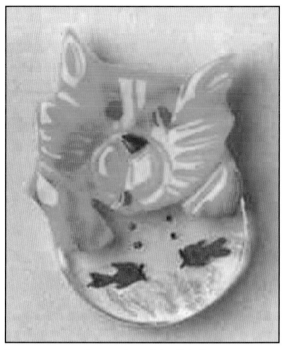

Adorable carved cat pin in Tequila Sunrise Bakelite, with inset eyes. Lucite fishbowl with reversed carved and painted fish and water plants. 2-3/4". $425. Barbara Wood.

In contrast, another version of the Bakelite cat with a Lucite fishbowl pin. Note the slightly different technique used for the cat's eyes, and that the fishbowl features two fish. 2-3/4" across. $425+. Private collection.

These two ABC pins are made incorporating vintage Bakelite alphabet cubes. Clearly the cubes in these two pins are from several different sources. When you work with vintage materials, as the Shultzes do, you have to be willing to be flexible and utilize whatever you have available — which in the case of the Shultzes is constantly changing. Periodically they will have shortages or even completely run out of a certain color. At these times, their output will reflect this. A good example is that in the last few years, as transparent Applejuice Bakelite has become scarcer and correspondingly expensive, Ron and Ester have utilized it more sparingly.

Made from recycled Bakelite alphabet dice, this similar school theme pin has subtle differences from the other pin. Barbara Wood

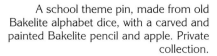

A school theme pin, made from old Bakelite alphabet dice, with a carved and painted Bakelite pencil and apple. Private collection.

One-of-a-Kinds

In essence all Shultz pieces are one-of-a-kind. But some are more one-of-a-kind than others. Some pieces, such as the experimental "compulsive art" pieces that Ron does on a whim, are absolutely once in a lifetime Shultz Bakelite events. Sometimes, because of the rarity of some of the materials used in a piece, that piece can never be duplicated exactly the same way again. There are a few techniques, which, once accomplished, Ron and Ester swear that they are unwilling to ever attempt again. Occasionally, Ron and Ester will make a piece in one of their familiar designs, but then tweak it in a special way, such as adding dots to it or making it only once in a certain color combination. These subtle nuances are part of what determines a one-of-a-kind piece. Some Shultz Bakelite designs are enduring, such as their classic checkerboard bangles, and they will probably be making them for some time to come. But some Shultz designs are made for only a short period of time and then they are retired and will not be made again. One example of a retired design is the beloved confetti bangle. As of this writing, Ron and Ester have stated that they will not be making any more of them.

An orange Bakelite flamingo pin, with a red laminated beak and black eye. Private collection.

In contrast, a blue-moon Bakelite flamingo pin, with a laminated red beak and black and white eye. Private collection.

What does a Shultz Bakelite diva wear on her wedding day? This incredible early one-of-a-kind Bakelite and Lucite bangle! This bangle appeared in my first book, *Bakelite Bangles Price and Identification Guide*. At that time, it belonged to a collector who had loaned it to be photographed. Sometime later, I managed to convince her to part with it. When I was dressing for our wedding, I informed my future husband that of course I would be wearing Shultz with my wedding dress (a fabulous handmade, handprinted silk traditional Moroccan caftan). I asked him to choose what he wanted me to wear with my wedding dress, and he chose this bangle. Henceforth, we have called it "the Wedding Bangle". The center sections are Lucite, and include two blue-moon compensation pieces. The Lucite is dotted with multicolored marbled confetti dots, and then the bangle is bordered on both sides with Paprika marbled borders. This is one of the great ones. 1-3/4" wide, 3/8" walls. $2000+. Karima Parry.

A Few Words about the Captions

The pieces shown in this book belong to a number of generous collectors both acknowledged and anonymous, as well as the author, and to the Shultzes. In general, the owner of each piece supplied information about the pieces shown. Using the information supplied to me by each collector and the Shultzes, I have made every effort to describe pieces accurately and completely. However, sometimes, for one reason or another, complete information on a piece was not available or a collector did not want to disclose it. In that case, rather than exclude the piece, I elected to include it with whatever information I was able to obtain because I want to show as much of the breadth and variety of the Shultzes' work in this book as possible. I ask the reader's indulgence on any captions that are incomplete.

The owner of each piece determined its pricing. On some seemingly similar pieces, the reader may note that at times that there is significant variation in pricing. This could be due to several factors including the rarity of that particular piece; the inclusion of especially rare colors of Bakelite in that particular piece, the intricacy of the craftsmanship or the use of special techniques, what that collector paid for that piece, and occasionally the affection with which the collector regards that particular piece. Arguably, in the eyes of their owners, some of the pieces in this book are priceless. I would therefore remind the reader that the prices given here are only a rough guide. In addition, Shultz Bakelite jewelry has been appreciating in value and the prices in this book reflect the prices that prevailed at the time this book was written.

Finally, there is the sometimes sticky matter of attribution. Shultz Bakelite is bought and sold and pieces attributed to one collector may have changed hands by the time this book is in print or afterwards. So, the attribution of pieces in this book to any given collector reflects who owned the piece at the time that this book was written, and may no longer be the case.

Pricing Shultz Bakelite Jewelry

There are many factors that go into determining prices for Shultz Bakelite jewelry. First of all, they are handmade, signed works of art, and they each have their own value as pieces of art. Secondly, although almost all Shultz pieces are predominantly made of Bakelite, some kinds and colors of Bakelite are more rare and precious than others, and pieces that include them would reasonably be valued higher than pieces composed of other more common colors and kinds of Bakelite.

In purely practical terms, after materials costs, the most important consideration is the amount of labor in each individual piece. A Scottie pin that is sliced from rod and detailed obviously would have fewer hours of labor in it than an intricately reverse-carved and painted bangle.

The next factor would be rarity. Certain pieces are made in multiples, almost as limited edition production pieces. These would obviously be less rare, and less valuable, than one-of-a-kind pieces. Also, it has been the tendency of the Shultzes in the past to make certain designs for a period of time, and then to stop making them. Therefore, those pieces which are no longer being made appreciate in value over time, as they are examples of pieces that are in very limited supply.

Finally, although more a problem at the production end than for collectors, the waste factor must be considered. No matter how much material the piece contains at the end, prior to finishing a certain percentage of it was ground, sanded, or cut away as waste. This unrecoverable waste Bakelite was a part of the materials cost of the piece, and is factored into the price.

An oversized one- or few-of-a-kind Bakelite heron pin, with laminated beak and glass eye. $650+. Karima Parry.

A Work of Art

When you buy a piece of Shultz Bakelite jewelry, not only are you acquiring something that you can wear and enjoy, you are buying a handmade, signed work of art. It is never easy to put a price on a work of art. The usual formula of materials + labor + a reasonable profit just doesn't apply. When you buy a work of art, you are buying a piece of that artist's creative life. The span of that entire creative life can be a few short years or a lifetime. But the output of any artist can usually be placed along a timeline from early to middle to later. In considering the value of a piece of art, to begin with it is important to place it within the context of that artist's total output to date.

If it's an early piece, created at the beginning of the artist's evolution, by definition it would be somewhat exploratory and experimental. As the artist learns, pieces from their early period reflect that and their own development. During the transition from early to middle period, when an artist begins to become established and their style becomes codified and their work known, the naivete and abandon of early pieces is usually transcended as the artist begins to arrive at what works for them. Earliest pieces can sometimes reflect experiments that didn't work, and spontaneous accidents that will never happen again. For a serious collector of the work of any artist, there is a special cachet to owning the earliest pieces. They are the benchmark of that artist's beginnings.

Pieces from the middle period of an artist's output usually show the maturation of their vision and their creative style, as well as their growing mastery of whatever medium and tech-

A one-of-a-kind oversized Bakelite horse head pin, with laminated black mane, glass eye, and painted detail. $600+. Karima Parry.

niques they have chosen to employ. Middle pieces have a sureness that early pieces lack. The trade off, however, is that they often lose the spontaneity and creative exuberance of early pieces. Often as an artist becomes established and their unique vision translates to their own personal style, their middle period pieces assume almost a "production" quality. Through trial and error they have learned what works, what sells, and what doesn't, and middle period pieces are made to sell. Many artists produce the largest volume of work during their middle period. The best of the middle period pieces generally form the backbone of any serious collection. They exemplify what that artist is most known for and what they do best.

At some point during the middle period, it seems that some artists arrive at a transformative period where they begin to experiment once more. Having mastered their medium and techniques, established themselves and their work, they have earned a freedom to rethink their work. Later pieces are about legacy. They are the culmination of the artist's creative voyage, and in the later pieces the artist finally can concentrate completely on saying what they want to say, and upon pleasing no one except themselves. They are the summation of their artistic life and expression, and their final statements as artists.

What this has to do with Shultz Bakelite is to remind us that over the years that the Shultzes have been creating Bakelite jewelry their art has gone through years of refinement and change. From their first button necklaces to the truly dazzling checkerboard bangles and virtuoso pins of late, Ron and Ester have evolved as craftspeople and as artists. By placing their pieces in context in terms of their age the collector is given a window into the Shultzes' own creative process and their development as artists, and does have some impact in terms of valuing each piece.

Material — Not All Bakelite Is Equal

In the early days, Ron and Ester began making Bakelite jewelry by cutting up all sorts of items that were originally made of Bakelite. They still do. Ester informed me that the wonderful horse head and bird pins on the previous page were made from cutting up a 1930s jukebox.

But Bakelite has not been manufactured to its original recipes for over fifty years, and all the Bakelite that exists is already out there. As collecting interest has risen dramatically in the last few years, Bakelite is starting to be scarcer than it was before. Ron and Ester buy Bakelite for making their jewelry when and where they can, and they have a limited stock of blank bracelets as well as rod, sheet, and other forms of raw Bakelite. Replenishing their stock is increasingly costly and difficult, and Ron and Ester completely run out of certain colors from time to time.

Applejuice and other transparent Bakelite have become especially scarce and prices for it have risen to the point that, in 2000, Ron and Ester started charging a surcharge for checkerboards which include transparent material. Prices for reverse-carved bangles are also rising with no ceiling in sight, as the blanks to produce them are becoming increasingly pricey and scarce.

As stated earlier, some kinds of Bakelite are especially rare and more valuable than others. Stardust Bakelite, a special favorite of the author, was manufactured only for a one-year period, spanning 1936-1937, making it among the rarest of Bakelite. Any Shultz piece that is made of or incorporates Stardust would be especially valuable.

Purple Bakelite is rare, and exists in shades from pale orchid all the way to deep midnight purple, and everything in between. Shultz pieces that are purple or include purple Bakelite command a premium. The same is true to for aqua and turquoise, and, to a lesser extent, for pink. Also especially desirable are unusual marbled colors.

So, in pricing Shultz pieces, two otherwise identical two-row checkerboard bangles can vary greatly in price if one of them is in opaque green and black, and the other is in purple and Applejuice. The later can be worth as much as 50% more than the former!

And don't get the mistaken idea that the few Lucite Shultz pieces out there are worth much less than the Bakelite pieces because they are Lucite and not Bakelite. Because of their scarcity, and because the labor intensity is the same whether the Shultzes are working in Bakelite or Lucite, Shultz Lucite pieces command prices that are only slightly less than comparable pieces in Bakelite.

Waste

The crafting of any piece of Bakelite jewelry includes a certain percentage of waste. The reason is that during the final sanding, polishing, and finishing processes every piece will lose a certain amount of Bakelite, which will be ground into dust. Unlike working in gold or silver where the dust can be recaptured and recycled, Bakelite dust cannot be recycled and is absolutely worthless. But this lost Bakelite is still a part of the materials cost in that piece.

Some techniques are especially wasteful to create. Among them, Belle ovals, double Belle ovals, and checkerboard bangles stand out. Part of the higher cost for pieces incorporating these techniques is because of the high rate of material loss in producing them. Because the Shultzes prefer to be frugal with the material, these and other techniques that are especially wasteful of material will only be made in very limited quantities.

Labor

It stands to reason that the more hours of labor in a piece, the more the piece should cost. This is another reason for the high cost of reverse-carved and painted pieces. They require hours of labor, and take more time to make than a carved pin, for example. Over the years, the Shultzes have most likely developed some assembly line techniques for producing multiples of certain styles of pieces. For example, when Ester is making reverse-carved and painted dotted bangles, it is highly likely that she will be working on more than one at the same time. This can result in some marginal savings of time and labor, but there are few shortcuts that will result in any substantial lowering of the amount of labor in the pieces. One of the reasons Ron and Ester stopped making confetti was that it was simply too labor intensive, with each dot requiring several separate steps to complete. In general, therefore, the more dots on a piece, the more techniques on a piece, the more labor on a piece, the higher the value of that piece.

Rarity

Although every Shultz piece is handmade, some are created in multiples. Usually that multiple pattern is only made for a short period of time. A good example would be the red, white, and blue commemorative pieces that Ron and Ester made for a short time in the wake of the events of September 11, 2001. Others include subtle differences from piece to piece. For example, a waterfowl pin may exist plain, or exactly the same as the plain one but with a laminated beak, or with a glass eye, laminated beak and wing, etc. Or the famous pelican pin with the laminated beak where each example of the pin is laminated in a slightly different order of colors. In general, though, the more embellished the piece, the rarer it is, and the higher its value. The Shultzes have made quite a few checkerboard bangles, but three-row checkers are rarer than two-row checkers, because fewer of them exist, and because they have announced that they will not be making any more of them; they are simply too wasteful of material.

Only a few collectors are fortunate enough to acquire pieces that are especially unique. Ron's "compulsive art" pieces are highly coveted treasures for collectors. However, within the realm of multiples, few-of-a-kinds, and one-of-a-kinds, the determinant can be that the piece is done in different colored Bakelite than all the other pieces made in that design. Sometimes it is a question of its size or scale, or that it is more embellished than other pieces in that design. All of these factors can determine a unique piece. Whenever a piece is a one of a kind, its value rises significantly. "Compulsive" pieces are almost impossible to price, and the fortunate collectors who have them consider them to be priceless.

Appreciation

Shultz Bakelite jewelry is definitely appreciating in value for a variety of reasons. The first reason is that the material it is made from, Bakelite, has risen dramatically in price over the past few years. The second reason is that the Shultzes have gained recognition and respect as bona fide artists and their work has attracted a growing body of devoted collectors. As their reputation grows, it is reasonable to expect that demand for their wonderful pieces will continue to increase, while the number of pieces available will always definitely be limited. Many Shultz collectors refuse to part with their Shultz pieces, so the number of older pieces that reach the market is very limited. And, the Shultzes have a very limited capacity to produce new pieces, so supplies of them will also always be very limited.

Patterns and Techniques

Basic Construction

Pins: Some Shultz pins are made from blanks that are sliced off from vintage Bakelite pin rods, which were made pre-cast in various shapes. However, most Shultz pins are sawed out and constructed.

Bangles: Some Shultz bangles are made from vintage Bakelite bangle bracelet tubes, from which blanks of any width can be sliced. Other Shultz bangles are made by modifying vintage Bakelite bangles.

Constructed bangles: Some Shultz bangles, such as checkerboards, are completely constructed from pieces of Bakelite that are laminated together and formed into a bracelet.

Techniques

Lamination: One piece of Bakelite is joined to another by precisely fitting the area where the two pieces will meet. Glue is applied, and then the joined area is clamped until it dries.

Layered lamination: Some Shultz pieces are made with lamination that is layered, with one lamination on top of another.

Dots

Confetti: Round flat dots of varying sizes, usually in groups.

Wraparound dots: Round or oval dots which are shaped to a convex curve, with the middle of the curve flush across the top of the dome on a bangle.

Fingernails: an elongated irregular oval-shaped dot that narrows at one end.

"Belle Kogan" ovals (also known "Belle" ovals): Named in honor of Belle Kogan, an early Bakelite designer who was especially fond of elongated ovals. She did a series of bangles with elongated ovals of various sizes laid on their sides and laminated all around the bangle.

Overlay dotting: When two dots are deliberately placed so that one overlaps the other. "Double Belles" are two "Belle Kogan" ovals in which a smaller one is carefully overlaid one a larger one. Another kind of overlay dotting are "bull's eye dots," which are a special kind of precision overlay dotting, where a smaller dot is fully overlaid over a larger one so that it sits in the exact center of the dot below it.

Carving

Surface carving: Carving that appears on the front of the piece only.

Reverse carving: Used on pieces made of transparent Bakelite or Lucite only, this is carving on the back of a piece or the inside of a bangle so that it shows through the piece and can be viewed from the front.

Additional Decorative Techniques

Painting: Small accents are occasionally highlighted with paint.

Reverse painting: Painted accents added on the inside of reverse-carved areas, such as coloring in reverse-carved fish.

Laminate decorations: A very small decorative accent, such as the eye of a bird pin, which is laminated.

Foreign decorative materials: Leather, plastic covered string, glass eyes, etc.

I consulted with Ron and Ester to place the techniques listed below in order by degree of difficulty, the least difficult first, and escalating to the most difficult. After each technique, I have noted who does which techniques:

Lamination - Ron
Belle Ovals - Both
Wraparound Dots - Ron
Fingernail Dots - Ron
Double Belle Ovals - Both
Carving - Ester
Piercing - Ester
Painting - Ester
Reverse Carving - Ester
Confetti Dotting - Ron
Checkerboards - Ron, Ester, and their daughter Eve
Injection Dotting - Ron

There is an undeniable link between vintage Bakelite jewelry and Shultz pieces. The Shultzes have utilized some of the styles that are commonly found in vintage Bakelite. But rather than revive vintage designs, the Shultzes have used them as an inspirational springboard. By reinterpreting them rather than reproducing them, they have taken their pieces out of the traditional vernacular and placed themselves and their work firmly in a later era than vintage Bakelite jewelry.

Confetti

Two stacks comprising eight confetti-dotted Bakelite bangles in various colors and widths. In general, the bigger the bracelet and the more numerous the dots, the higher the price. However, rare colored blanks such as the orchid marbled one on top of the right hand stack, and rare colored dots, such as purples, aquas, and pinks, will raise the value of a confetti bangle, as will overlapping or bull's eye dots. $450-850, each. All Karima Parry.

Dotting

A stack of four rarer colored dot Bakelite bangles. From the bottom, fuchsia pink with six black wraparound dots, 1/2" wide, 3/8" walls, $475-550. Karima Parry. Next, a laminated pink-bordered robins egg blue octagon with black dots. This is a rarer bangle, possibly one-of-a-kind. 1" wide, 5/16" walls, $800-950. Private collection. A one-of-a-kind translucent raspberry with four shocking pink Belle ovals, with black dots. 1/2" wide, 3/8" walls, $600-750. Karima Parry. On top, a one-of-a-kind deep turquoise with four double Belle ovals, shocking pink-over-black, 1/2" wide, 3/8" walls, $600-750. Karima Parry.

When Ron started making dots of various sizes, and scattering them all over the bracelets in random patterns they named this technique and pattern "Confetti." As confetti evolved, the size of the dots varied from very small to quite large. As Ron became more proficient at dotting, he began to experiment with overlapping the edges of the dots, and then laying one dot on top of another. Confetti bangles that include overlaid dots and bull's eye dots are especially coveted by collectors.

The Shultz's dotting technique has evolved over time. Ester told me that the first dotted pieces "... had dime-sized dots." Next, Ron zigzagged them around the bracelet. Many of the earliest Shultz polka dotted bangles were made utilizing very wide and chunky Bakelite "balloon" bangles. The most common bangle colors were Creamed Corn and Leaf Green. A few blue ones exist, as well as a few in other colors.

A classic early Shultz four-dot Bakelite bangle featuring four oversized pink marbled dots on a wide green "balloon" blank. 1-5/8" wide, 3/8" walls. $750-900. Helene Lyons.

Another early Bakelite balloon bangle with very large dots. 1-3/4" wide, 3/8" walls. $600+. Ron and Ester Shultz.

An apricot marbled Bakelite bangle, with the black dots arranged in an unusual zigzag pattern. 7/8" wide, 5/16" walls. $500. Private collection.

A married pair of white Lucite bangles with Bakelite dots. On one bangle, the dots are arranged in diagonal stripes. On the other, the dots are sprinkled all over the bracelet in a random pattern. The Shultzes have made few confetti bangles in Lucite and they are uncommon. 1-7/8" wide, 3/16" walls, each. $850-950 for the pair. Private collection.

Earlier ivory "balloon" Bakelite bangle with red dots laid out in a uniform pattern. 1-3/4" wide, 3/8" walls. $550. Barbara Wood.

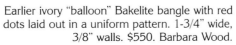

A married pair of ivory Bakelite bangles with black confetti dots laid out in a regular pattern. The larger is 1-1/2" wide. $650-700. The smaller is 1/2" wide with 1/4" walls. $300. Barbara Wood.

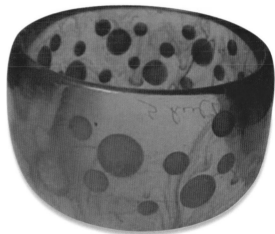

An early tea-colored Bakelite bangle with random sized yellow confetti dots in a random pattern. 1-1/2" wide. 1/4" walls. $700. Barbara Wood.

Random sized and random patterned confetti dots on a wide, green marbled Bakelite bangle. Private collection.

A very early rainbow confetti-dotted Bakelite bangle. 1-3/4" wide, 1/4"+ walls. $550. Ron and Ester Shultz.

Another early rainbow confetti-dotted Bakelite bangle. 1-1/2" wide. $550. Barbara Wood.

An early rainbow confetti-dotted Bakelite bangle in an unusually colored greenish yellow. 1-1/2" wide. $600. Barbara Wood.

An early rainbow confetti-dotted Bakelite bangle in moss green with cream swirls. 1-1/4" wide, 3/16" walls. $550. Barbara Wood.

A fuchsia pink Bakelite ultra-wide confetti bangle. 1-7/8" wide. $800. Jenaay Brown.

An early exceptionally wide rainbow confetti-dotted Bakelite bangle. 2-3/8" wide, 1/4" walls. $800. Barbara Wood.

An applejuice Bakelite bangle, with rainbow confetti dots. Transparent confetti bangles are scarce and are especially desirable. 15/16" wide, 1/4" walls. $800. Barbara Wood.

Three tube bangles with confetti dots. The applejuice with rainbow confetti is especially desirable. 1/2" wide, 3/8" walls. $550. A matched pair of yellow and ivory tube bangles, with multicolored dots. 3/8" wide, 3/8" walls, each. $300, each. Barbara Wood.

A huge stack of white Bakelite bangles with rainbow confetti dots. 1/2" wide, 1/4" walls, each. $300-400, each. Barbara Wood.

Black Bakelite rainbow confetti-dotted bangles are scarce. This one is 1" wide, with 3/8" walls. $650. Barbara Wood.

A black Bakelite bangle, with rainbow confetti dots. 1-1/4" wide, 5/16"+ walls. $500. Ron and Ester Shultz.

Two one-of-a-kind Bakelite bangles with rainbow confetti dots. The pink is 1-1/8" wide, 3/8" wall $450-550. The orange is 1" wide with a 3/8" wall. $400-500. Private collection.

An early grey-blue balloon Bakelite bangle covered with rainbow confetti dots in various sizes, many overlapping. 1-1/2" wide, 3/8" walls. $750-900. Helene Lyons.

An exceptionally wide blue-moon Bakelite bangle with confetti dots in all colors and sizes. 1-3/4" wide x 3/8" walls. $750. Barbara Wood.

An early dark green Bakelite balloon bangle with lots of multicolored confetti dots, including some overlapping. 1-5/8" wide, 3/8" wall $750-850. Private collection.

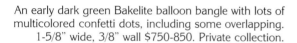

An early Bakelite balloon bangle, with rainbow confetti. Private collection..

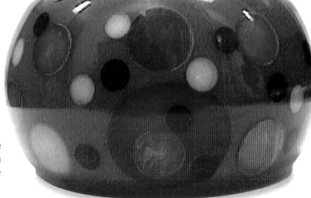

An exceptionally nice early forest green balloon Bakelite bangle covered with rainbow confetti dots, many overlapping and a few bull's eyes. 1-5/8" wide, 3/8" walls. $850-1000. Helene Lyons.

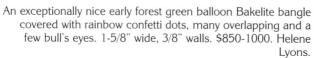

A combination dotted Bakelite bangle. Rainbow confetti accents a few strategically placed large, slightly oval dots. 1-1/8" wide, 3/8" walls. $550. Ron and Ester Shultz.

A rare bordered confetti-dotted Bakelite bangle. Barbara Wood.

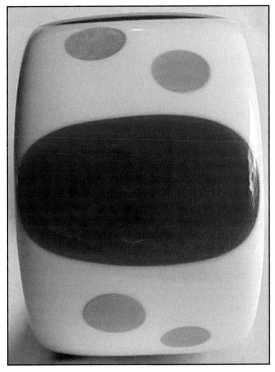

A very wide ivory Bakelite bangle with four oversized oval dots accented with small, lime green confetti dots. 1-7/8" wide, 5/16" walls. $500. Barbara Wood.

Heavy one-of-a-kind gray Bakelite bangle with dots, ovals, stripes and some squares. 1-3/4" wide, 3/8" walls. $600. Barbara Wood.

Another rare bordered Bakelite confetti-dotted bangle. Barbara Wood.

An unusual Bakelite bangle with oversized dots alternating with bull's eye dots. Barbara Wood.

Laminated black and clear Bakelite with red, yellow, and green confetti dots. 15/16" wide, 3/8" walls. $800. Barbara Wood.

An wonderful older pair of heavily rainbow confetti-dotted Bakelite bangles. These were pink when they were originally made, however these days they have oxidized to a pale orange with butterscotch overtones. 1-1/4" wide, 5/16" walls, each. $500+, each. Barbara Wood.

A pair of wide black Bakelite rainbow confetti-dotted bangles. 1-1/2" wide, each. $1000, each. Jenaay Brown.

Two creamed corn Bakelite "balloon" bangles of different vintages, each embellished with multicolor confetti dots. The "super confettied" bracelet in the foreground is a later piece, whereas the bracelet in the background is an earlier one. This can be determined by comparing the oxidation level of the dots on both pieces. The piece in the rear is clearly substantially more oxidized, which suggests that it is older. In general, when considering confetti bangles, the more confetti, the more desirable (and higher priced) the piece. The upper "super confettied" bangle would be considered one of the best confetti bangles. 1-3/4" wide, 3/8" walls, each. Upper bangle $950, lower bangle $750+. Private collection.

Wraparound Dots

Ron soon mastered the technique of making dots that were deeply set into the material spanning the width of the bangle. They were polished off so that they curved along with the dome of the bangle, instead of sitting flat and flush as Confetti dots do. These dots were named "wraparound dots," and mastering the technique of making them enabled the Shultzes to produce their own version of the well-known vintage Bakelite "6-dot" bangles and to make variations on that theme.

It is especially interesting to note that the wraparound dots can vary in size and proportion, and, when placed on bangles of various proportions, many different looks are achieved.

A married stack of three light celadon green marbled Bakelite bangles. All measure 1/2" wide, with 3/8" walls. The bottom one is one-of-a-kind, and has four black dots unusually placed within laminated sections. $650+. Private collection. The middle one has fourteen dots in black, red, yellow, and green. $550. Karima Parry. The top bangle has six dots alternating navy blue and cherry marbled. $450. Private collection.

Two rare colored, marbled Bakelite six-dots; a purple marbled on custard, and an ink blue marbled on camphor, both with black wrap-around dots. 1/2" wide, 3/8" walls. $600 each. Karima Parry.

A married pair of jade marbled Bakelite bangles, one with six black wraparound dots, the other with eight black wraparound dots. 1/2" wide, 3/8" walls, each. The pair: $850-900. Karima Parry.

An oppositional pair of Bakelite "six-dot" bangles. A burgundy-moon with blue-moon wraparound dots, and blue-moon with burgundy-moon wraparound dots. 5/8" wide, 3/8" walls, each. $800-900 for the pair. Private collection.

A stack of three six-dot Bakelite bangles in black and yellow. The top one is a rare black and white marbled. This stack is one of the author's favorites! 1/2" wide, 3/8" walls, each. $1200-1350 for all three. Karima Parry.

Very rare! Purple marbled Bakelite, each with six petal pink wraparound dots. 1/2" wide, 3/8" walls. Center bangle slightly flying saucer-shaped. $1400-1550+ for all three. Karima Parry.

Turquoise Bakelite is rare! The wider bangle has yellow confetti dots, and is 15/16" wide, with 3/16" walls. $550. Barbara Wood. The bottom one is 9/16" wide with 3/8" walls. $600. Karima Parry.

A married pair of Bakelite oppositional dotted bangles. Black with white wraparound dots is 1/2" wide with 3/8" walls. $600. White with black wraparound dots is 5/8" wide with 3/8" walls. $800. Barbara Wood..

Transparent dotted Bakelite bangles are especially desirable. Of these two applejuice Bakelite bangles, the bottom one has six black wraparound dots, $500, and the top one has eight black wraparound dots. $650. Although when they are first completed they look clear, they will soon re-oxidize back to a golden applejuice color. 5/8" wide, 3/8" walls, each. Barbara Wood.

A rare transparent peach Bakelite bangle with eight black wraparound dots. $800. An applejuice Bakelite bangle with six black wraparound dots. $600 Both are 5/8" wide, 3/8"+ walls. Karima Parry.

Two pairs of Bakelite six-dot bangles. Transparent red, and transparent orange, all with black wraparound dots. 1/2" wide, 3/8" walls, each. $1000-1150 per pair. Karima Parry.

A matched pair of marbled tea, swirled with powdered Stardust Bakelite bangles. Each bangle has eight wraparound dots in marbled pastel colors. 1/2" wide, 3/8" walls, each. $1000, the pair. Karima Parry.

A married pair of very rare one-of-a-kind rootbeer swirled Bakelite bangles, each with twelve wraparound Stardust dots. The darker bangle is 7/16" wide, the lighter one is 1/2" wide, both have 5/16" walls. $1000+ for the pair. Karima Parry.

These are the narrowest Shultz bangles I have ever seen. A matched trio of teenie weenie wraparound dotted six-dot Bakelite bangles. 1/4" wide, 1/4" walls. All three: $400-500. Private collection.

A pair of Bakelite tube bangles with dots. 3/8" wide, 3/8" walls, each. $300 each. Barbara Wood.

Two rarer twelve-dot, sliced shaped bangles. On the bottom, a one-of-a-kind jade and milk marbled Bakelite bangle with rare burgundy swirled applejuice dots, 3/8" wide, 3/8" walls, $425-550. On the top, a cherry vanilla dotted Lucite sliced bangle, 3/8" wide, 3/8" walls, $400-475. Karima Parry.

A stack of three citron Bakelite bangles, each with six wraparound dots. Private collection.

Two pairs of six-dot yellow marbled Bakelite bangles. The brighter lemon ones are dotted in marbled orange, 5/8" wide, 3/8" walls, each. The softer yellow ones are dotted in marbled aqua. 1/2" wide, 3/8" walls. $950 each pair. Karima Parry.

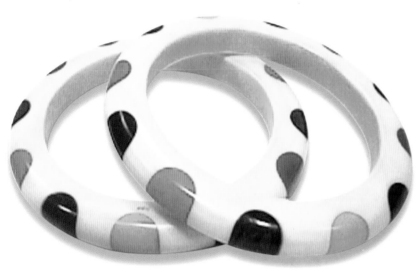

A matched pair of creamed corn Bakelite bangles, each with twelve multicolored wraparound dots. 3/8" wide, 3/8" walls. The pair: $1100-1300. Karima Parry.

Unusually colored white with green marbling Bakelite bangle with 8 large orange wraparound dots. 5/8" wide, 3/8" walls. $450-500. Marcia Rybak.

Gaudy marbled brown with cream and turquoise dots. 3/4" wide, 3/8" walls. $600. Barbara Wood.

A pair of Bakelite bangles, each with (rare) purple wraparound dots. 5/8" wide, 3/8" walls, each. $650-800, each. Orange marbled, private collection. Green marbled, Karima Parry.

A matched set of three transparent tea marbled Bakelite bangles with wraparound dots. One with yellow dots and two with turquoise dots. Turquoise is a rarer color, and therefore especially desirable. 3/4" wide, 3/8" walls, each. $375-450 each. Private collection.

A married pair of Bakelite bangles with alternating red and black wraparound dots. The upper bangle has the dots arranged in a straight row, but the lower bangle has the dots arranged in an up and down pattern. Both are 5/8" wide, 3/8" walls. $550-650, each. Ron and Ester Shultz.

A citron Bakelite bangle with six hot pink wraparound dots, and six oversized navy wraparound dots. 5/8" wide, 3/8" walls. $500-600 Lori Kizer.

Extra large, cream-colored Bakelite tube bangle with twelve large black wraparound dots. This is a rare bangle. 5/8" wide with 5/8" walls. $650. Barbara Wood.

An unusually large applejuice Bakelite tube bangle with eight oversized black wraparound dots. 1/2" wide with 1/2" walls. $600+. Barbara Wood..

A pair of transparent Prystal Bakelite bangles with wraparound dots. Rare turquoise with eight aqua marbled dots, 13/16" wide, 3/8" walls. $850. Karima Parry. Cherry red with six pink swirl dots. 7/8" wide, 3/8" walls. $650. Barbara Wood.

"Belle" Ovals

Ron and Ester developed their own oval-shaped dots, which are usually set on their sides. In honor of Belle Kogan, these are known as "Belle" ovals. Ron took them a step further when he overlaid them with a second smaller oval, creating "Double Belles."

Collectors have named the 1/2" wide, 1/4" wall transparent bangles that usually have four "Belle" ovals "Candy bangles" because of their resemblance to hard candies. A few especially rare ones exist which are covered with confetti dots.

A group of five Bakelite bangles, each with variations on "Belle" ovals. On the left, a pair of oval and dot bangles. 5/8" wide, 3/8" wide, each. $400-500, each. On the right on the bottom is a rarer bangle with laminated ovals. 1-3/8" wide, 1/4" wall. $750-900. On the right on the top is an orange "fried egg" double "Belle" oval bangle, 3/4" wide, 3/8" wall. $475-625. On the top is a rare one-of-a-kind mosaic double "Belle" oval bangle. 5/8" wide, 3/8" wall. $600-750. Private collection.

Orange Bakelite bangle with four large "Belle" oval dots in various colors. 1" wide, 1/4" walls. $325. Barbara Wood.

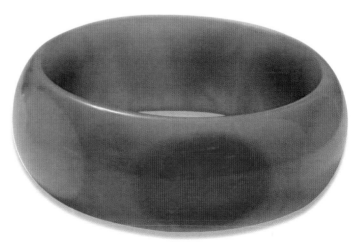

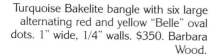

Turquoise Bakelite bangle with six large alternating red and yellow "Belle" oval dots. 1" wide, 1/4" walls. $350. Barbara Wood.

Rootbeer Bakelite bangle with six large yellow "Belle" oval dots. 1" wide, 1/4" walls. $350. Barbara Wood.

Red Bakelite bangle with four large "Belle" ovals in yellow, black, green and orange. 1" wide, 1/4" walls. $350. Barbara Wood.

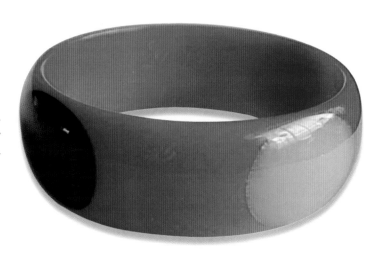

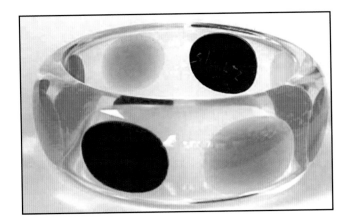

Lucite bangle with alternating red, green, and black Bakelite "Belle" oval dots. 1-1/2" wide, 3/8" walls. $600. Barbara Wood.

Bright shocking pink Bakelite bangle with alternating oversized electric blue and black "Belle" oval dots. 1" wide, 5/16" walls. $350. Barbara Wood.

In this group of "Belle" ovals bangles, the ovals are laid out in a zigzag pattern instead of in a straight line as in the previous group. A red Bakelite bangle with six large yellow zigzagged "Belle" ovals. 1" wide, 1/4" walls. $350. Barbara Wood.

Burgundy-moon Bakelite bangle with six white "Belle" oval dots in a zigzag pattern. The ovals will eventually oxidize to ivory. 1" wide, 5/16" walls. $450. Barbara Wood.

Very chunky tea-colored Bakelite bangle with turquoise marbled "Belle" oval dots in a zigzag pattern. 1-1/8" wide, 3/8" walls. $450. Barbara Wood.

On a very chunky citrus yellow Bakelite bangle, eight oversized black "Belle" ovals in a zigzag design. 1-1/4" wide, 3/8" walls. $550. Ron and Ester Shultz.

Each of these three "Belle" oval bangles are special. Rare gaudy marbled turquoise Bakelite bangle with eight large pink "Belle" oval dots. 7/8" wide, 3/8" walls. $750. Barbara Wood.

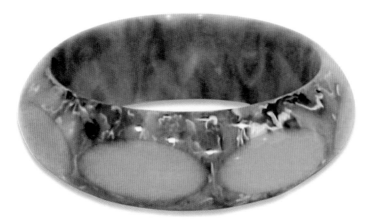

A rare one-of-a-kind Stardust rootbeer swirl Bakelite bangle, with seven large sea green marbled "Belle" ovals all around. 7/8" wide, 3/8" walls. $850-950. Karima Parry.

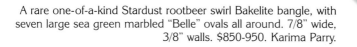

A very special one-of-a-kind Stardust applejuice Bakelite bangle, with four large purple "Belle" ovals floating along the surface. Stardust, which was manufactured for only one year (1936-1937) features tiny to large shreds or flakes of gold suspended inside the Bakelite and is an extremely rare material. Purple is rare too, so, this Shultz which is made entirely out of rarer Bakelite material is especially desirable. Another one of the author's favorites! 1" wide, 5/16" walls. $1000+. Karima Parry.

Overlapping "Belle" ovals are not common, making all the bangles in this group especially desirable. A Bakelite bangle with overlapping "Belle" ovals, multicolored. Private collection.

A Bakelite bangle with overlapping "Belle" ovals, multicolored. Private collection.

A chunky Bakelite bangle with overlapping multicolored and variously sized "Belle" oval dots. 1-1/8" wide, 3/8" walls. $500-600. Ron and Ester Shultz.

43

A matched "go together" set of Bakelite bangles with a very rare and unusual center bangle. It is pink with large overlapping multicolored "Belle" oval dots. 1" wide, with 3/8" walls. The set includes two tube bangles in pale blue with matching "Belle" oval dots. 3/8" wide, 3/8" walls, each. The set: $1,800. Barbara Wood.

Pale pink Bakelite bangle with large red rounded square (or squared oval?) dots. 1" wide, 1/4" walls. $325. Barbara Wood.

An unusual colored café au lait Bakelite bangle with large chocolate sundae marbled "Belle" ovals. 5/8" wide, 3/8" wall. $450-500 Private collection.

A matched set of five milk marbled Bakelite tube bangles. Each has four "Belle" ovals in pastel colors. These were not acquired together. They were collected from various sources one at a time. 3/8" wide, 3/8" walls. All five: $1350-1500 Private collection.

A pile of Bakelite bangles with "Belle" oval dots. Several of these are on rarer colored blanks. The top bangle is camphor with blue marbling, with six "Belle" ovals in marbled colors including pink, yellow, lavender (rare), and cherry vanilla. 5/8" wide, 3/8" walls. $600. Karima Parry. In the center, an uncommon cafe au lait colored bangle with large "Belle" ovals 1/2" wide, 3/8" walls. $600. Private Collection. On the bottom right, a very unusual turquoise with chocolate marbling bangle, with deep teal ovals. 1/2" wide, 3/8" walls. $550 Karima Parry. On the bottom left, a marbled white with four large ovals. 1/2" wide, 3/8" walls. $500. Private collection.

A trio of Bakelite bangles, each with "Belle" ovals all around. On either side, rare turquoise with rare purple and fuchsia ovals. 5/8" wide, 5/16" walls. $1000 the pair. In the center, chartreuse green with four ovals, 5/8" wide, 3/8" walls. $450. Ron and Ester Shultz.

A group of three Bakelite bangles, each with four huge "Belle" ovals, and one which also has four wraparound dots. The middle bangle is a rarer opaque mauve color. The top bangle is an unusual cafe au lait color, and two of the ovals on it are purple and deep fuchsia pink. 3/4" wide, 3/8" walls, each. $450-700 each. Private collection.

Transparent Bakelite or Lucite bangles with "Belle" ovals have a special allure. The ovals appear to be suspended in space. This may be one of the reasons that they are especially desirable for Shultz collectors, and a little more expensive than ovals on translucent or opaque bangles. An applejuice Bakelite bangle with four alternating pastel yellow and lavender "Belle" ovals. 1/2" wide, 3/8" walls. $500. Marcia Rybak.

An extra chunky married pair of applejuice Bakelite bangles, each with pastel marbled "Belle" ovals in Easter pastels: pink, lavender, yellow, and green. 9/16" wide, 7/16" walls, each. $550-675 each. Karima Parry.

When "Belle" ovals are combined with dots on transparent bangles, the effect is magical. A rare transparent lavender Bakelite bangle, with pink marbled "Belle" ovals alternating with confetti dots. 1/2" wide, 1/4" walls. $450. Marcia Rybak.

A stack of narrow applejuice Bakelite bangles, each with multicolored pastel "Belle" ovals and wrap-around dots. 3/8" to 1/2" wide, 3/8" walls, each. $450-550, each (lizard not included). Marcia Rybak.

An extra chunky married pair of applejuice Bakelite bangles, each with marbled "Belle" ovals. One has four blue-moon ovals, the other has six sea green marbled ovals. 9/16" wide, 3/8" walls, each. $550-675 each. Karima Parry.

From the bottom, a transparent wine Bakelite bangle with alternating aqua marbled and tangerine marbled "Belle" ovals. 3/4" wide, 3/8" walls. $500-650. A transparent peach juice Bakelite flying saucer with chalk blue "Belle" ovals. 3/8" wide, 3/8" walls. $400-450. Another transparent wine Bakelite bangle with aqua marbled "Belle" ovals. 3/4" wide, 3/8" walls. $500-650. And on top, an unusually colored transparent vaseline Stardust Bakelite bangle with chalk blue "Belle" ovals. 1/2" wide, 7/16" walls. $650-800. All pieces Karima Parry.

A rare transparent lavender Bakelite bangle, with four fuchsia pink "Belle" ovals, and four fuchsia pink dots. 1/2" - wide, 1/4" walls. $450. Ron and Ester Shultz.

On a narrow applejuice Bakelite bangle, black "Belle" ovals alternate with small black confetti dots. 3/8" wide, 5/16" walls. $400. Ron and Ester Shultz.

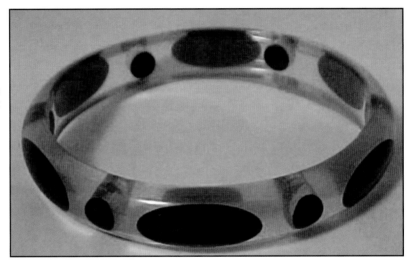

A charming married pair of applejuice Bakelite bangles, each with four tangerine "Belle" ovals alternating with four lime green marbled dots. The only difference between the two bangles is the size of the lime green dots. 9/16" wide, 3/8" walls, each. $900-1100 for the pair. Marcia Rybak.

A married stack of three transparent red Bakelite bangles, each with marbled "Belle" ovals in pastel colors. The center bangle has small yellow marbled polka dots in between each "Belle" oval. All are 5/8" wide, with 3/8" walls. $500-650, each. Karima Parry.

A married stack of three transparent green Bakelite bangles, each with marbled "Belle" ovals in pastel colors. The top bangle also has small red marbled polka dots. Top and bottom bangle each measure 5/8" wide. the center bangle, which also has milky marbling and the ovals butted end to end, is 1/2" wide. All have 3/8" walls. $500-650, each. Karima Parry.

Shultz lovers can get lost in the subtle patterns within marbled bangles, and with marbled double "Belle" ovals, the gaudier the marbling, the better! Marbled turquoise Bakelite bangle with double "Belle" ovals of aqua marbled over white. 5/8" wide, 1/4" walls. $650-700 Marcia Rybak.

A jade marbled Bakelite bangle, with four matching double "Belle" ovals of burgundy underneath with marbled purple on top. 3/4" wide, 3/8" walls. $600-750 Karima Parry.

A matched pair of celadon marbled Bakelite bangles, each with four double "Belle" ovals including various combinations of marbled greens, purple, pink, lavender, and aqua. 1/2" wide, 3/8" walls. The pair: $1000-1200 Karima Parry.

On the bottom, a burgundy-moon Bakelite bangle with alternating double "Belle" ovals all around. Two are green marbled over white, and the other two are fuchsia pink-over-white. 1/2" wide, 3/8" walls. $550. Private collection. On top, a rare pale apricot marbled Bakelite bangle, with chalk blue-over-lavender purple double "Belle" ovals all around. $600. Karima Parry.

Wonderful opaque Bakelite bangles with double "Belle" ovals have their own special impact. A very rare deep turquoise opaque Bakelite bangle, with four fuchsia pink-over-black double "Belle" ovals all around. 1/2" wide, 5/16" walls. $650 Karima Parry.

Bright orange Bakelite bangle with double "Belle" oval dots in blue-moon-over-white. 3/4" wide, 3/8" walls. $550-650. Barbara Wood.

A "go together" matched set. In the center, a chunky tangerine Bakelite bangle with yellow-over-aqua double "Belle" ovals. 1" wide, 3/8" walls. On the edges, a pair of tangerine Bakelite tubes with alternating yellow and aqua "Belle" ovals. 3/8" wide, 3/8" walls. The set $1250. Ron and Ester Shultz.

A pair of chunky Bakelite bangles , each with four oversized double "Belle" ovals. 1"+ wide, 3/8" walls, each. $650-750, each. Ron and Ester Shultz.

Big double "Belle" ovals are big impact! A rare turquoise Bakelite bangle with four huge red-over-white double "Belle" oval dots. As you can see from the way the collector photographed her treasured bangle, to Shultz collectors the beauty of the unadorned Bakelite itself is as important to them as the areas which have been decorated with dots. 1-1/2" wide, 1/4" walls. $700-800. Private collection.

Wide blue Bakelite bangle with four huge double "Belle" oval dots in red-over-white laid vertically, as opposed to horizontally on the bangle. 1-1/2" wide, 1/4" walls. $700-800. Judith Black Gale.

Carnelian marbled Bakelite bangles. Each has burgundy-moon-over-aqua double "Belle" ovals alternating with lime marbled wraparound dots. 3/4" wide, 3/8" walls, each. All three $1500-2000. Barbara Wood, who tells me that this is one of her favorite stacks.

A group of the author's favorite double "Belle" oval Bakelite bangles. All marbled, eight in various widths and colors. In general, prices rise depending on the size of the bangle, and whether any rarer colors such as purples, aquas, or pinks are present either in the dots, or the bangle itself. Widths range from 1/2" to 1", all have 3/8" walls. $500-850, each. Karima Parry.

A stupendous stack of seventeen transparent Bakelite "candy" bangles in a variety of colors including rare ice blue, lavender, Stardust vaseline, pink, green, and applejuice. Each with four marbled "Belle" ovals in a variety of colors. 1/2" wide, 1/4" walls, each. $300-350 each, except the Stardust ones which are $350-400, each. Karima Parry.

A pair of rare transparent aqua Bakelite "candy" bangles, each with four pastel marbled "Belle" ovals. 1/2" - wide, 1/4" walls. $650, the pair. Karima Parry.

A very rare pair of transparent antifreeze green Stardust Bakelite "candy" bangles, each with four "Belle" ovals. 1/2" - wide, 1/4" walls. $750, the pair. Karima Parry.

A group of three transparent Bakelite "candy" bangles, including a rare lavender one, each with four "Belle" ovals in various colors. 1/2" - wide, 1/4" walls. $1000 for all three. Karima Parry.

A matched pair of transparent hot pink Bakelite "candy" bangles. Both are embellished with black, red marbled, and blue-moon confetti dots. Confetti decorated candy bangles are unusual. Normally, the Shultzes decorate candy bangles with "Belle" ovals. 1/2" wide, 1/4" walls, each. The pair, $650- 750. Private collection.

A group of multicolored transparent Bakelite "candy" bracelets, each overlaid with four "Belle" ovals. 1/2" wide, 1/4" walls, each. $250-350, each. Private collection.

Fingernail Dots

Making dots which are oval, and not round presented special challenges first to make and then to inlay because of their irregular elongated shape. When they finally mastered this especially difficult kind of dotting, Ron and Ester made bangles with these dots, which came to be known as "fingernail dots." Fingernail dotted bangles are difficult to make, and the Shultzes did not make many of them. They are rare, labor intensive, and expensive.

A stack of six opaque colored Bakelite bangles, each with a double row of fingernail dots. Various widths and colors. $900-1100 each, with the aqua one (also seen on the cover) being slightly higher because it is a very rare color. Karima Parry.

An unusual wide yellow Bakelite bangle. The middle row is alternating long yellow and smaller black checks, while the borders are embellished with black fingernail dots. 1-3/4" wide, 3/8" walls. $900. Barbara Wood.

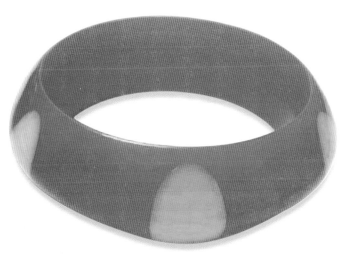

A red Bakelite flying saucer bangle, with interesting rounded triangle shaped bright yellow fingernail dots along the perimeter. 1" wide with 3/8" walls. $600. Barbara Wood.

A rust red swirled Bakelite bangle, with two rows of smaller sized black fingernail dots. 1-1/4" wide, 1/4" walls. $900. Barbara Wood.

A one-of-a-kind applejuice Bakelite bangle with two rows of fingernail dots — one red and one black. 1" wide, 1/4" walls. $900. Barbara Wood.

A matched pair of chunky Bakelite bangles, in pink and in green, each with two rows of black fingernail dots. 1-1/8" wide, 3/8" walls, each. $1400-1500 for the pair. Private collection.

A wild stack of Bakelite bangles with unusual fingernail dotting. Two have a single row of fingernails, each, laid on the diagonal all around the bangles. The one of the bottom has the fingernail dots laid in a zigzag pattern. 1"+ wide, 3/8" walls, each. $750-850 each. Ron and Ester Shultz.

A rare, one-and-only translucent tea color Bakelite bangle with two rows of small fingernail dots. 1/2" wide, 5/8" walls. $1,000. The bottom bangle is gaudy marbled browns with black dots. $450. Barbara Wood.

A very special masterpiece, one-of-a-kind applejuice Bakelite bangle (will re-oxidize back to golden yellow in time) with two rows of closely spaced black fingernail dots all around. Thirty-eight dots total. 5/8" wide, 3/8" walls. $2000+. Barbara Wood.

A pair of chunky narrow Bakelite bangles, each with two rows of fingernail dots. 1/2" wide, 7/16" walls. $1500 the pair. Ron and Ester Shultz.

Injection Dotting (also known as Bow Ties)

The dotting "tour de force" in Bakelite is making injected dots. Making these dots is so demanding because modern injected dot pieces must be constructed, whereas on vintage pieces, rods were injected into the pieces, creating dots when the plastic was hot, prior to it being cured. Making "bowtie"-shaped injected dots today is a delicate and laborious process. Parallel tunnels are drilled out from one edge of the bangle to the other, and precisely measured pieces of rod are carefully inserted and laminated into the drilled areas. These are then cut off and polished.

Ester commented, "Ron has done several bow tie bracelets where he has drilled the bracelet through and inserted the bows from one side to the other. This the most difficult technique to do, and that is why they are not common. If you find one of those you have a very special bracelet that only exists in very limited quantities. He has done a few here lately that have turned out wonderfully." Shultz injected dot bangles are rare and pricey, and there will never be many of them.

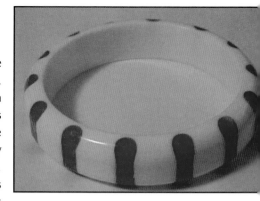

A one-of-a-kind white with pink marbled Bakelite injected bowtie-ish rods bangle. 1/2"+ wide, 5/16" walls. $1250+. Karima Parry.

Two rare black Bakelite injected dot bangles. Although the one on the left is clearly not as thick as the one on the right, because injected dots are so rare, width and wall thickness are not significant in determining price. $1,000+ each. Barbara Wood.

A rare red with green and black "injected dot" bowtie Bakelite bangle. 3/4" wide, 5/16"+ walls. Private Collection.

A rare Bakelite bow tie "injected" dot bangle. Navy blue, with red, yellow, and green dots. 3/4" wide, 3/8" walls. $900-1100. Private collection.

Rare one-of-a-kind cream corn Bakelite bangle with dense "injected dot" bowties. 9/16" wide, 3/8" walls. $2,000+. Barbara Wood.

Rare yellow with red "injected dot" bowties Bakelite bangle. 7/8" wide, 3/8" walls. $1,200. Barbara Wood.

Rare black Bakelite "injected dot" bowtie bangle with red, green, and yellow bowties. 3/4" wide, 5/16" walls. $1000-1150 Marcia Rybak.

Very rare lime green with very tightly laid black "injected dot" bowties Bakelite bangle. 7/8" wide, 1/2" walls. $1,500+. Barbara Wood.

Combination Technique Pieces

Combination techniques pieces are those upon which the Shultzes have "gilded the lily," utilizing multiple techniques, sometimes with one technique overlaying another. All of the decorative techniques that the Shultzes use are labor intensive, but when combination techniques are employed, not only is the artistic impact of the piece raised to a whole new level, in practical terms, the amount of labor in the piece is increased dramatically. Combination technique Shultz jewelry, therefore, is especially desirable, and higher priced than single technique pieces.

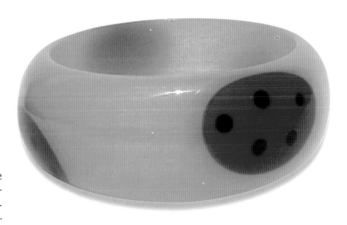

On a very chunky Citron Bakelite bangle, red-over-green double "Belle" ovals are inlaid with tiny black confetti dots, creating watermelon slices, complete with seeds! 1-1/8" wide, 3/8" walls. $750-850. Private collection.

Combination Dotting

The Shultzes have made pieces that incorporate multiple dotting techniques on a single piece. These include bangles such as the ones that alternate "Belle" ovals with wraparound dots.

Two Bakelite bangles, each with four large marbled "Belle" ovals and four wraparound dots. The larger is lime marbled and is 7/8" wide, 3/8" walls. $500-600. The narrower is chartreuse and is 1/2" wide, 3/8" walls. $500-550. Karima Parry.

A stack of seven unusual and rarer colored bangles, in various colors and widths, all with "Belle" ovals and wraparound dots, in various combinations. From the top, cream marbled with chocolate; Inkspot (camphor marbled with deep teal blue); pale yellow marbled; spinach marbled; "snot" green marbled; deep opaque raspberry; apple jade marbled. $400-750. Raspberry, Private collection. All others, Karima Parry.

Ovals are taken to a higher level when they are dotted, composed of laminated stripes, or composed of checkerboard. A matched "go together" pair of chunky rootbeer Bakelite bangles. Each is circled with cream "Belle" ovals. On the lower bangle, the "Belle" ovals are doubled with marbled black over the cream. On the upper bangle, the ovals are overlaid with marbled black dots $1,200-1,350, the pair. Lori Kizer.

A matched "go together" set of three chunky Bakelite bangles. The center bangle has oversized "Belle" ovals which are inlaid with multicolored confetti dots. 1"+ wide, 3/8"+ walls. On either side are a matched pair of wraparound dotted bangles in matching colors that complement the center bangle. 5/8" wide, 3/8" walls, each. Shultz "go together" sets are prized by collectors. $2,000. Barbara Wood.

A stack of three large chunky Bakelite bangles. Each has oversized "Belle" ovals which are inlaid with small confetti dots. 1-1/4" wide, 3/8" walls, each. $1,000 each. Barbara Wood.

Special Techniques Dotting

Special techniques in dotting are when more than one technique is utilized on a single dot. These include "Belle" ovals that are then overlaid with polka dots, dots that are themselves made from delicate sandwiches of laminated slivers of Bakelite, or small ovals entirely made of checkerboard. Because they are extremely labor intensive, as well as uncommon, special techniques dotted bangles are especially desirable for Shultz Bakelite collectors, and are more expensive.

On a chunky Bakelite bangle, "Belle" ovals are horizontally laminated with multicolored stripes. Possibly one-of-a-kind. 1" wide, 3/8" walls. $750-800. Private Collection.

A very rare chunky turquoise with cream marbling Bakelite bangle, with four "Belle" ovals which are made of fuchsia pink and marbled transparent rose Bakelite checkerboards. Entirely made of rarer colors, and absolutely one-of-a-kind. 1" wide, 3/8" walls. $900+ Karima Parry.

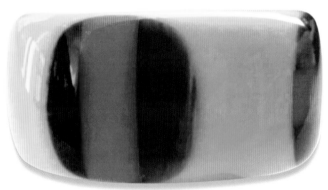

Laminated ovals are rare. Bright yellow Bakelite bangle with four large dots composed of laminated multicolored stripes. Alternating around the bangle, each dot is inlaid in a different direction. 1-1/2" wide, 1/4" walls. $750-850. Barbara Wood.

Pale pink Bakelite bangle with large rainbow ribbed laminated dots, and scattered with small pink confetti dots throughout. Measures 1-14" wide, 1/4" walls. $900. Frances Cavaricci (who told me that she bought it for her daughter who loves pink).

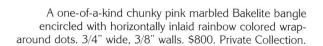

A one-of-a-kind chunky pink marbled Bakelite bangle encircled with horizontally inlaid rainbow colored wrap-around dots. 3/4" wide, 3/8" walls. $800. Private Collection.

Checkerboard "Belle" ovals are rare, labor intensive, and pricey. Pink Bakelite bangle with purple and aqua marbled checkerboard "Belle" ovals alternating with lime green dots. The color combination on this piece is particularly striking. 7/8" wide, 1/4" walls. $900-1100. Marcia Rybak.

Two chunky Bakelite bangles, each with large oval checkerboard dots. The blue is the more desirable of the two because of the rarity of blue bangles. 1-1/4" wide, 3/8" walls, each. $1,000-1150, each. Barbara Wood.

A stack of three very chunky opaque Bakelite bangles, each decorated with four checkerboard "Belle" ovals. 1"+ wide, 7/16" walls, each. $1000 each. Ron and Ester Shultz.

The ultimate checkerboard "Belle" ovals Bakelite bangle. On this amazing one-of-a-kind piece, over a chunky red blank, a series of one-of-a-kind checkerboard "Belle" ovals are overlapped all around. 1" wide, 3/8"+ walls. $1500+ Private Collection.

Laminated Bangles

Laminated bangles are made from layers of Bakelite sandwiched together. The more layers, the more desirable the piece. In addition, some laminated bangles are overlaid with dots or other decorative techniques. The ones featuring dotted double ovals that look like watermelon slices are especially desirable.

A jumble of laminated Bakelite bangles. Averaging 1" wide with 3/8" walls. $450-550, each. Ron and Ester Shultz.

A five-layer laminated Bakelite bangle with burgundy-moon, white marbled, and blue-moon layers. 1" wide, 5/16" wall. $450-550 Private collection.

A pair of laminated five-layer Bakelite bangles. Shocking pink with white marble, and lemon yellow with white marble. 1" wide, 5/16" walls, each. $900-1100 for the pair. Private collection.

A married pair of burgundy-moon and pink laminated five-layer Bakelite bangles. On the left: 1-1/8" wide 1/4" walls. $400-550. Right: 1" wide 1/4" walls. $400-550. Private collection.

A rare seven-layer laminated Bakelite bangle. 1" wide, 5/16" walls. $600. Barbara Wood.

A multicolored seven-layer laminated Bakelite bangle. 1" wide, 5/16" wall. In judging laminated bangles in general, the more layers, the higher the price. $650-700 Private collection.

A milk marbled and black five-layer laminated Bakelite bangle, with watermelon sliced dots. This bangle is probably a one-of-a-kind. 1" wide, 3/8" walls. $800-950. Karima Parry.

Older five-layer laminated Bakelite bangle in ivory and orange, overlaid with large watermelon slices made of red-over-green double "Belle" ovals, which are then sprinkled with tiny black confetti dots. There are very few watermelon bangles around, and even fewer that are done on laminated bangles. 1" wide, 5/16" walls. $800. Barbara Wood.

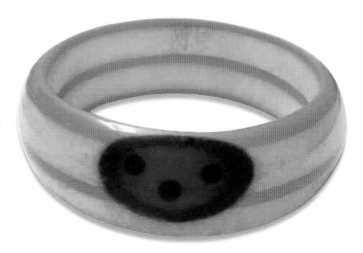

Ribs

The "ribs" bangles are a relatively new Shultz design. Over an interior liner bangle, domed ribs of Bakelite are butted together in a row that completely encircles the bangle. On a few rare pieces, the ribs are laid diagonally. A few dotted pieces also exist where the dots are comprised of ribs.

A pair of ribbed-over-black Bakelite bangles. The upper bangle is done in bright colors, the lower one in pastels. 1"+ wide, 3/8"+ walls, each. $1000+, each. Barbara Wood.

Multicolored Bakelite ribs, arranged upon a black Bakelite blank. In rib-patterned bangles in general, the more the ribs, the higher the value of the bangle. Extra value is also added for rarer colored ribs. 1" wide, 3/8" walls. $900. Private collection.

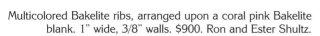

Multicolored Bakelite ribs over a black Bakelite bangle. 1" wide, 7/16" walls. $900. Barbara Wood.

Multicolored Bakelite ribs, arranged upon a coral pink Bakelite blank. 1" wide, 3/8" walls. $900. Ron and Ester Shultz.

This is very special! Multicolored pastel Bakelite ribs, arranged upon a rare Stardust Bakelite blank. Note the translucency of the bangle, and how the colors of the ribs can be seen from the inside. $1000+. Barbara Wood.

Multicolored Bakelite ribs over a pink Bakelite bangle. 1" wide, 7/16" walls. $900. Barbara Wood.

Multicolored pastel Bakelite ribs arranged on a coral pink Bakelite blank. 1" wide, 3/8"+ walls. $900. Ron and Ester Shultz.

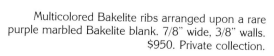

Multicolored Bakelite ribs arranged upon a rare purple marbled Bakelite blank. 7/8" wide, 3/8" walls. $950. Private collection.

On a rare turquoise Bakelite bangle, very rare "Belle" oval dots diagonally laminated with multicolored ribs spaced all around in a zigzag layout. 1" wide, 5/16" walls. $1000+. Private collection.

On an extremely rare purple marbled octagon-shaped Bakelite bangle, multicolored Bakelite ribs are arranged diagonally all the way around. 7/8" wide, 3/8" walls. $950. Private collection.

A "go together" matched set. A rootbeer Bakelite octagonal bangle with angled ribs laid in a chevron pattern. 1" wide, with varying wall thicknesses up to 9/16". $800-900+. Pair of marbled light green Bakelite mini tubes each with eight wraparound black cherry dots. 3/8" wide, 3/8" walls, each. $450-550 for the pair. All pieces, Lori Kizer.

Chunks

Derived from ribs, a few Shultz pieces feature very large protruding chunks of Bakelite laminated around the perimeter of a bangle or combined with other techniques.

A pair of purple marbled Bakelite bangles with large "chunks" all around in pink, purple, yellow, blue, and orange. 9/16" wide, 5/8" walls. These are unusual, both for their purple liners and because few pairs of chunk bangles seem to exist. $2500. Judith Black Gale.

Checkerboards

Arguably, if the Shultzes have a signature piece or signature technique, it's their meticulously crafted checkerboard bangles. In many ways, Shultz checkerboard bangles represent a considerable achievement in Bakelite craftsmanship.

To begin with, they require a certain shape of Bakelite as their raw material, and that particular kind of Bakelite only exists in increasingly limited quantities. This can limit the color choices or amounts of certain colors that appear in checkerboard bangles. Further, Ron and Ester have told me that the crafting process for making checkerboards wastes large amounts of the material. So the colors and material allocated to an individual checkerboard must be carefully planned in advance of construction.

Making checkerboard bangles involves constructing a checkerboard that is symmetrical and matches up properly between each square, and shaping that checkerboard into a bangle is convex on the exterior and then sharply and uniformly curved along the reverse to create the interior. Construction must be incredibly precise. Early Shultz checkerboards illustrate that this is not such an easy task, as they often include "compensation piece;" that is, pieces of Bakelite inserted at the end of the fabrication of the bracelet when the layout did not quite come out evenly. Shultz collectors especially treasure these early checkerboards as they have a charming quirkiness. Later checkerboards are dazzling because of their stunning precision.

Ron Shultz.

A very exceptional early red and black Bakelite three-row checkerboard bangle, with checkered borders. Including the borders, this bracelet has an amazing five rows of checkers. Constructed over a translucent grey liner. 1-3/4" wide, 3/8" walls. $1300-1800 Helene Lyons.

A number of the earliest Shultz checkerboard bangles were constructed by laminating the checkerboard onto a "liner" bracelet. Later checkerboards have utilized liners less often. During the time that the Shultzes made predominantly "lined" checkerboard bangles, transparent Bakelite rarely appears in the checkerboards. After all, its transparency would be wasted because the lining prevents much of the light from passing through the Bakelite. However, with honing of their construction techniques, the "liner" has gradually been dispensed with. This has allowed the creation of checkerboard bangles that include transparent Bakelite. These have become especially sought after by collectors, and they continue to command a premium over checkerboards that only consist of opaque Bakelite. One reason for this is the contrast of opaque and transparent Bakelite is particularly suited to the checkerboard design. Another reason is that obtaining transparent material for checkerboard bangles is difficult; the material is rare and getting rarer. As a result, Ron and Ester are forced to charge a special surcharge on checkerboard bangles that include transparent Bakelite.

Constructed over an ivory Bakelite liner bangle, with creamed corn borders; a row of laminated multicolored checkers. This is an early prototype and is a one-of-a kind. Measures 1-3/4" wide, 3/8" walls. $800. Barbara Wood.

An early Bakelite checkerboard bangle. Red and yellow checks constructed over a yellow liner, with black borders. 1-7/8" wide, almost 3/8" walls. $1,200. Barbara Wood.

A very early Bakelite checkerboard bangle. Red and blue checks constructed over a butterscotch swirl liner, with butterscotch borders. 1-3/4" wide, 3/8" walls and slightly larger than 2-1/2" inside. $1,200. Barbara Wood.

An early three-row checkerboard bangle in transparent red and black Bakelite. Measures 1-3/8" wide, with 3/8" walls. Note that the checks are not precisely uniform in size, and don't quite match up, and a smaller "compensation piece" has been inserted. Early checkerboard bangles such as these are highly sought after. $1800-2000. Barbara Wood.

Two early one-of-a-kind lined Bakelite checkerboard bangles in black and white. The first is constructed over a black liner, with black borders and especially precisely laid smaller checks. This bangle is very heavy and chunky. 1-1/2" wide, 1/2" walls. $1500+ Barbara Wood.

The second older one-of-a-kind black and white Bakelite large checks checkerboard bangle has unusual rounded checked borders. 1-1/4" wide, 1/2" walls. $900-1200. Barbara Wood.

This is an early two-row checkerboard bordered red and black Bakelite that is constructed over a translucent Bakelite liner bangle. 1-3/8" wide, 3/8" walls. $950-1250. Helene Lyons.

A later one-of-a-kind prototype four-row checkerboard Bakelite bangle. The liner bangle inside is white, while the outside includes clear red and clear checks that will change to light applejuice as they re-oxidize. Slightly under 2" wide, with 3/8" walls. $1,200. Barbara Wood.

Ron and Ester have a very special helper who sometimes assists them in making checkerboards. It is their daughter, Eve. Ester is justifiably proud of her daughter. "To add to your checker story let me tell you about Eve. Eve has been a missionary for about 11 years now. She has spent many years in Spanish speaking countries such as El Salvador, Ecuador, and now for the last two years she has been in Mexico. She is an ordained street minister who specializes in ministering to little children. While she was here in the United States on a break between missions two years ago she stayed here with us for a year and in that year decided she wanted to get involved in our work and help us some."

"Ron spent a while showing her how to build the checkerboard bracelets and she caught on quickly. We have tried to teach others how to do this but they have never seemed to be able to master the technique. But Eve learned fast and soon was a great blessing to us. She does an excellent job and has become very quick at it. She builds the bracelet and Ron finishes it and makes it into the super checkerboards that you see today. She comes home about three times a year and in that time makes as many checkerboards as she has time to do. She has a great eye for precision and she does quality work."

In judging checkerboard bangles, desirability is determined by several criteria. Early checkerboards are prized, but very rare. In later checkerboards size, proportions, and material are the most important considerations in establishing their value. In checkerboards, the bigger the better. Three-rows are generally more valuable than two-rows, and the chunkier and heftier they are, the higher the price. There are, of course, those petite collectors who prefer the narrower, less chunky two-rows to the very chunky walled oversized ones, which can be quite heavy to wear. Material is also an important consideration. As previously mentioned, transparent Bakelite is more valuable than opaque. Applejuice is especially desirable. Also, rare colors, such as aqua, rouge flambe (red with black marbling), and purples in particular, raise the desirability and the price of individual checkerboard bangles.

Eve Shultz.

Two-Row Checkerboards

The most common Shultz checkerboard bangles are "two-row." They exist in a wide array of colors and proportions. A few two-rows exist which are flying saucer-shaped. These are among the rarest of the two-row checkerboard bangles.

A matched set of four two-row Bakelite checkerboard bangles, each with black, and a contrasting transparent color: cherry juice, pink, applejuice, and emerald. 15/16" wide, 3/8" walls, each. $750-850 each. Karima Parry.

A lovely group of three two-row checkerboard Bakelite bangles. On the highest end of the price scale are those that are all transparent, such as the one on the lower left. 7/8" wide, 3/8" walls, each. $750-1200 each. Private collection.

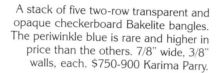

A stack of five two-row transparent and opaque checkerboard Bakelite bangles. The periwinkle blue is rare and higher in price than the others. 7/8" wide, 3/8" walls, each. $750-900 Karima Parry.

This piece and the next three show variations of two-row checkerboard bangles in various combinations of black, white, gray, and transparent. Gray with white swirl and transparent Bakelite two-row checkerboard bangle. 15/16" wide, 3/8" walls. $1500. Barbara Wood.

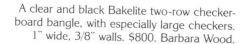

A clear and black Bakelite two-row checker-board bangle, with especially large checkers. 1" wide, 3/8" walls. $800. Barbara Wood.

A black and white Bakelite two-row checker-board bangle. 1" wide, 3/8" walls. $1000-1200. Jenaay Brown.

A rare black with white swirl and light gray with white swirl Bakelite two-row checker-board bangle. 15/16" wide, 3/8" walls. $1200-1400. Judith Black Gale.

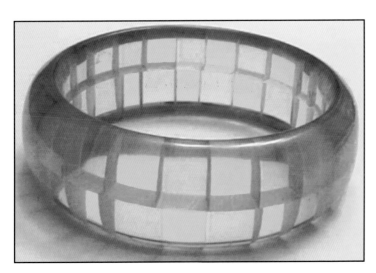

Transparent citron and clear Bakelite two-row checker-board bangle. 7/8" wide, 3/8" walls. $1000-1200. Barbara Wood.

A two-row Bakelite checkerboard bangle made from opaque yellow and opaque white Bakelite. Note the difference in price between this bangle and the preceding one, which is essentially the same color combination, except that the preceding bangle is in all transparent material. 1" wide, 3/8" walls. $700. Barbara Wood.

A very rare, overscaled two-row checkerboard bangle in black and applejuice Bakelite. 1-1/4" wide, 1/2" walls. $1,500. Barbara Wood.

An overscaled, unusual yellow transparent/translucent marbled and black two-row Bakelite checkerboard bangle. 1" wide, 1/2" walls. $1250. Ron and Ester Shultz.

Unusual clear Bakelite with lots of bubbles and "snot" green Bakelite two-row checkerboard bangle. 1" wide, 3/8" walls. $900. Barbara Wood.

A rare shade of lime green and applejuice Bakelite two-row checkerboard bangle. 1" wide, 3/8" walls. $1,200. Barbara Wood.

Two rarer two-row Bakelite checkerboard bangles. On the bottom is very chunky opaque brown and applejuice with rare larger sized checks. 1-1/4" wide, with scant 1/2" walls. $1,200. On the top is a marbled tea and applejuice 1-1/8" wide, 3/8" walls. $1,000. Barbara Wood.

The considerable difference in value between this bangle and the one below is because transparent peach juice is a rarer color than transparent tangerine. Transparent peach juice and opaque white two-row Bakelite checkerboard bangle. 7/8" wide, 3/8" walls. $1000-1200. Barbara Wood.

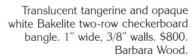

Translucent tangerine and opaque white Bakelite two-row checkerboard bangle. 1" wide, 3/8" walls. $800. Barbara Wood.

These two two-row checkerboard bangles are actually an oppositional pair. The first is transparent green and opaque yellow Bakelite. 7/8" wide, 3/8" walls. $1000-1200. Barbara Wood.

An opaque green and applejuice Bakelite two-row checkerboard bangle. The higher value of this bangle over the preceding one is because of the rarity of applejuice Bakelite. 15/16" wide, 3/8" walls. $1200-1400.

Two rarer colors: a marbled pink and applejuice Bakelite two-row checkerboard bangle. 15/16" wide, 3/8" walls $1500-1600. Barbara Wood.

A pink and opaque yellow Bakelite two-row checkerboard bangle. Note the difference in value with the preceding bangle. 1" wide, 3/8" walls. $1000-1200. Barbara Wood.

An extra chunky transparent applejuice and cherry juice Bakelite two-row checkerboard bangle. 1-1/8" wide, an astonishing 1/2" wall. $1000-1200 Private collection.

A transparent green and "rouge flambe" (a rare color) two-row Bakelite checkerboard bangle. 15/16" wide 3/8" walls. $1100-1300. Barbara Wood.

Rare color! Opaque iris blue with clear Bakelite two-row checkerboard bangle. 1" wide, 3/8" walls. $1000-1200. Karima Parry.

Large iris blue and applejuice Bakelite two-row checkerboard bangle. 1-1/8" wide, 1/2" walls. $1,200. Barbara Wood.

Two Bakelite checkerboard bangles. On the bottom, royal blue and transparent green. On the top, medium green with clear. 15/16" wide, 3/8" walls, each. $1000-1200 each. Barbara Wood.

A group of three multicolored, mixed opaque and transparent two-row checkerboard bangles. The first is a chunky two-row checkerboard in two shades of opaque, and transparent and opaque green. 1" wide, 3/8" walls. $1200. Private Collection.

The second is a two-row Bakelite checkerboard bangle in opaque royal blue, transparent pink and clear. 7/8" wide, 3/8" walls. $1000-1200. Barbara Wood.

The third is a two-row Bakelite checkerboard bangle in opaque red, white, and blue, and transparent green. 15/16" wide, 3/8" walls. $1000-1200. Barbara Wood.

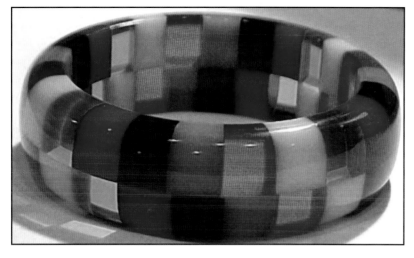

This is a wild multicolored transparent, translucent, and opaque, very chunky narrower two-row Bakelite checkerboard bangle. 7/8" wide, 3/8" walls. $1000+. Ron and Ester Shultz.

A very chunky two-row Bakelite checkerboard bangle which mixes multicolored opaque checkers with applejuice. 1" wide, 3/8" walls. $1000-1500. Barbara Wood.

A matched stack of two-row opaque black, yellow, green, and red Bakelite checkerboard bangles. The same bracelet, rendered in different colors and artfully combined makes a wonderful stack! 7/8" wide, 3/8" walls, each. $700-750, each. Bottom and middle bangles Karima Parry, top bangle Helene Lyons.

These are very rare! They each have a deep groove running along the center of the bangle. An opaque black and yellow, $950-1100; and a transparent red and opaque red, $1000-1250. Each measures 7/8" wide, with 3/8" walls. Both pieces Helene Lyons.

A group of three two-row checkerboard bangles. Each combines two shades of one color. The first is a pink marbled and translucent rouge flambe (rare color!) Bakelite. 1" wide, 3/8" walls. $850. Barbara Wood.

The second two-row checkerboard bangle combines deep pastel green with translucent camphor Bakelite, which takes on a greenish hue because of reflections from the green checkers. 1" wide, 3/8" walls. $1000-1200. Barbara Wood.

Among the rarest of two-row checkerboard bangles! A one-of-a-kind purple Bakelite two-row checkerboard bangle. Opaque fuchsia purple squares alternate with very rare translucent purple, lilac, and creme marbled squares. One of the author's absolute favorites. 7/8" wide, 3/8" walls. $1000+. Karima Parry.

This piece and the four two-row checkerboard bangles on the following page each combine a single color opaque with a single color of marbled Bakelite. The first one is pink swirl and royal blue. 1-1/4" wide, 3/8" walls. $1200-1400. Private collection.

Black cherry and marbled rose Bakelite two-row checkerboard bangle. 1" wide, 3/8" walls. $700-800. Lori Kizer.

Bright reddish orange and gray swirl Bakelite two-row checkerboard bangle. 1-1/4" wide, 3/8" walls. $1200. Private collection.

Royal blue and aqua swirled with chocolate milk Bakelite two-row checkerboard bangle. 15/16" wide, 3/8" walls. $1200-1400. Private collection.

Black and aqua swirl two-row Bakelite checkerboard bangle. 1" wide, 3/8" walls. $1000-1200. Barbara Wood.

Royal blue and marbled mango Bakelite two-row checkerboard bangle. 1" wide, 3/8" walls. $1200-1400. Private collection.

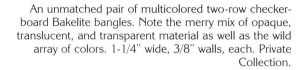

An unmatched pair of multicolored two-row checkerboard Bakelite bangles. Note the merry mix of opaque, translucent, and transparent material as well as the wild array of colors. 1-1/4" wide, 3/8" walls, each. Private Collection.

Orange and black with white marbling Bakelite two-row checkerboard bangle. 1" wide, 3/8" walls. $800 Barbara Wood.

An unusual color combination two-row checkerboard bangle made from grey, yellow, and purple Bakelite. 1" wide, 3/8" walls. $1200. Ron and Ester Shultz.

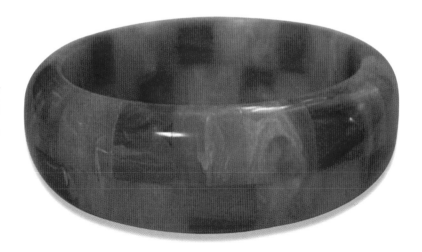

It's all about drama in these three rare overscaled two-row checkerboard Bakelite bangles. Not only are the proportions of the bangles overscaled, but the checkers they are made from are huge. The first is a combination of red opaque and clear Bakelite. 1-1/4" wide, 1/2" thick. $1,200. Barbara Wood.

The second two-row checkerboard bangle combines transparent green and clear Bakelite. Note the oversized checks. These larger sized check bangles are rare as only a few were made. $1500. Barbara Wood.

Rarest of this group, a blue-moon and applejuice Bakelite overscaled checkerboard bangle. 1" wide, 7/16" walls. $1200+. Lori Kizer.

Flying saucer-shaped two-row checkers are unusual and rare. This first is a one-of-a-kind, combines very large checks of rare material: rouge flambe and applejuice Bakelite. 1-1/8" wide, 1/2" walls. $1,000+. Barbara Wood.

The angles of this two-row rouge flambe and clear Bakelite flying saucer-shaped, two-row checkerboard bangle are a little steeper than the preceding bangle. 1-1/2" wide, 1/2" walls. $1500-1800. Barbara Wood.

A clear and rouge flambe Bakelite flying saucer shaped two-row checkerboard bangle. Note the especially steep slope of the outside walls on this piece. Very heavy, 1-7/8" wide, with 1/2" walls. $1,500-1,800. Barbara Wood.

On this most unusual flying saucer-shaped, two-row checkerboard Bakelite bangle, the blue checks are much narrower than the clear checks. Very heavy, 1-1/2" wide, 1/2" walls. $1500. Private collection.

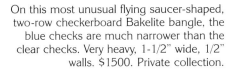

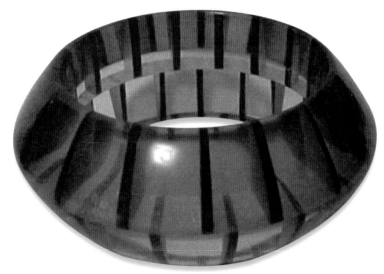

Three-Row Checkerboards

The lesser common Shultz checkerboards are "three-rows." They also exist in an array of colors and proportions. Some of the chunkiest ones are astonishingly heavy! Three-rows are definitely in limited supply. Ron and Ester stopped making them in late 1999, and have vowed that they will not make them again.

A stunning stack of three three-row checkerboard Bakelite bangles. 1-1/4" wide, 3/8" walls, each. The Shultzes have said that they will no longer be making three-row checkerboard bangles because they require such large amounts of material to make. Therefore, they are especially desirable. $950+, each. Private collection.

A rare rouge flambe and transparent mauve Bakelite three-row checkerboard bangle. $1500+. Private collection.

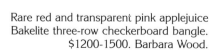

Rare red and transparent pink applejuice Bakelite three-row checkerboard bangle. $1200-1500. Barbara Wood.

The four on this page are three-row checkerboard bangles, each made entirely of opaque Bakelite. The first is in brown and ivory. 1-1/2" wide, 3/8" walls. Private Collection.

Older brown with cream swirls and cream colored Bakelite three-row checkerboard bangle. 1-3/8" wide, with 3/8" walls. There were only two made with these colors. $1800-2000. Kathleen Baker.

Brown with swirls of cream and a nice rich medium green Bakelite three-row checkerboard bangle. 1-3/8" wide, with 3/8" walls. I believe there were only two of this color combination made. $1800-2000. Kathleen Baker.

Red and green Bakelite three-row checkerboard bangle. 1-5/16" wide, 3/8" walls. $1,200. Barbara Wood.

On this page are four transparent Bakelite combined with black three-row checkerboard bangles. The first is in black and applejuice. 1-3/8" wide, 3/8 " walls. $850-950. Marcia Rybak.

A later black and transparent ruby Bakelite three-row checkerboard bangle. 1-7/8" x 3/8" walls. $1,200-1,500. Barbara Wood.

A rare black and applejuice Bakelite three-row checkerboard bangle. Note that the applejuice in this bangle is a different shade than that in the first bangle in this group. 1-7/8" wide, 3/8" walls. $1,500. Barbara Wood.

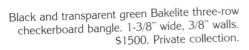

Black and transparent green Bakelite three-row checkerboard bangle. 1-3/8" wide, 3/8" walls. $1500. Private collection.

A three color opaque blue, pinkish Applejuice, and translucent camphor Bakelite three-row checkerboard bangle. 1-7/8" wide, 3/8" walls. $1,200-1,500. Barbara Wood.

An unusual three colored pinkish applejuice, black, and a very pale translucent coral Bakelite modified three-row checkerboard bangle. The coral is only used in the center row, creating a pattern within the checkerboard (and a pretty coral stripe on the interior). 1-7/8" wide, 3/8" walls. $1,000. Barbara Wood.

A three colored three-row checkerboard bangle, made of transparent red, transparent green, and opaque yellow Bakelite. Private collection.

Look carefully at these two three-row multicolor, mostly transparent Bakelite "rainbow" bangles. There are not many of these around, and each one appears to have a slightly different arrangement and selection of colors. 1-1/2" wide, 3/8" wall. $1050-1250. Private collection.

A mixed opaque, translucent, and transparent Bakelite three-row rainbow checkerboard bangle. Only a few of these exist, and there will not be any more made. 1-3/8" wide, 3/8" walls. $1050-1250. Karima Parry.

Bordered Checkerboards

Some checkerboards exist with plain contrasting borders. These can be a single row of checkers bound with narrow plain or checked borders all the way up to a three-row checker with borders.

Two bordered checkers. The first has yellow and clear Bakelite alternating checkers, bordered with yellow. 1-7/8" wide, 3/8" walls. $900 Barbara Wood.

This second bordered checker has alternating transparent red and yellow Bakelite checks with black borders. 1-3/4" wide 3/8" walls. $900. Barbara Wood.

An unusual, possibly earlier black and turquoise opaque Bakelite derivative checkerboard bangle. The center row has huge squares, which are flanked with plain black borders. 1-3/8" wide 1/4" wall. $750+. Private collection.

These may be a one-of-a-kind pair. A matched pair of bordered single-row checkerboard Bakelite bangles, with petal pink marbled squares alternating with transparent lavender, and transparent lavender borders. 3/4" wide 5/16" walls, each. $1150 for the pair. Private collection.

This pair is also possibly one-of-a-kind. A matched pair of Bakelite bordered checkerboard bangles. The center row is alternating squares of aqua and transparent lavender, with transparent lavender borders. 3/4" wide, 5/16" walls, each. $1150 the pair. Karima Parry.

A bordered checkerboard Bakelite bangle. Alternating opaque red and white checkers down the middle, with blue-moon borders. 5/8" wide, 3/8" walls. $550-650. Lori Kizer.

Derivative Checkerboards

Ron and Ester have also created a number of what i call "derivative checkerboards." These are totally constructed bangles that include checkerboard-type design and construction techniques, but feature checkered borders or other checkered elements, though not necessarily in the conventional arrangement of the usual two or three evenly sized rows of checkers. For example, a derivative checker might feature a larger central row of checkers flanked with narrower checkered borders.

The next step up from bordered checkers, is checkerboard borders. This is a one-of-a-kind bordered multicolored Bakelite checkerboard "Sampler" bangle. The center row has alternating squares of camphor and sea green. The borders are a merry mix of transparent, translucent, opaque, and marbled Bakelite in a wide variety of colors. 1" wide, 3/8" walls. $900-950. Karima Parry.

A wonderful variation, this is a one-of-a-kind unusual pink and mint green Bakelite checkered-border bangle with a center row of transparent Bakelite checkers. 3/4" wide, 3/8" walls. $750-875. Marcia Rybak.

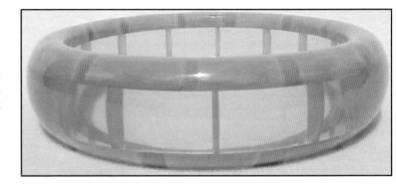

Unusual checkered-border checkerboard bangle. What makes this one special is that the center is a conventional pattern of alternating transparent green and clear Bakelite checks, while the borders alternate red checks with multicolored "slivers" checks. 7/8" wide, 5/16" walls. $850-950. Marcia Rybak.

One-of-a-kind older very wide three-row checkerboard in an unusual combination of colors including black, applejuice, yellow, and green Bakelite. $1500. Helen Zeve.

An earlier derivative checkered-border Bakelite checkerboard bangle. The center has two rows of random length multicolored thin rectangular checkers, and the borders are yellow and black checkers. Note that this is an early bangle, but it is not constructed over a liner. 1-3/8" wide, 5/16" wall. $950-1150. Private collection.

A later version of the previous derivative bordered Bakelite checkerboard bangle. On this bangle, the center has two rows of random length multicolored, thin rectangular Bakelite checkers, and the borders are red and black checkers. The proportions of this later bangle are chunkier than the preceding one. 1-1/4" wide, 3/8" wall. $900-1100. Private collection.

"Slivers" Checkerboards

On slivers-type checkerboard bangles, alternating squares of the checkerboard design are composed of tiny laminated slivers of Bakelite. On the finest slivers bangles, the individual squares are composed of four or more layers of slivers, however most are constructed of three layers of slivers. These are scarce and valuable.

One of the author's all time favorite Shultz bangles! A mosaic of Bakelite "slivers" in different sizes and colors, but predominantly blues and oranges. Absolutely one-of-a-kind. 1" wide, 3/8" walls. $1100+. Karima Parry.

Two versions of Bakelite "slivers" checkerboard bangles. On this first one, a two-row, transparent pink checkers alternate with multicolored marbled Bakelite "slivers" laminated together into checks. In valuing "slivers" bangles, the presence of rarer colors in the "sliver" squares, such as purples and aquas, brings them to the higher end of the price range, as does the number of pieces in the "sliver" checks. 7/8" wide, 5/16" walls. $850-950. Private collection.

A two-row Bakelite "Slivers" bangle. Transparent rose squares alternate with squares made up of three slivers of marbled Bakelite laminated together in random color combinations. Even more desirable are the few "slivers" bangles in which the colored squares are composed of four or more slivers. 7/8" wide, 3/8" walls. $900-950. Karima Parry.

Square Bangles

The Shultzes have made a very few square bangles. These are made in a variety of ways. Some of them are completely constructed, such as the one on the left in the first photo with the checkerboard liner. The corners are then built up with layers of lamination, forming a square bangle. Others appear to be made by starting with an octagon-shaped blank, and then building up four of the faces to create corners with successive layers of lamination. Finally, the squares are often decorated with dots. Square Shultz bangles are rare and unusual. They are very labor intensive as they combine multiple techniques, and prices on them will be high.

A group of six one-of-a-kind square Bakelite bangles. Each has laminated corners and dots on the sides. Private collection.

A group of four spectacular one-of-a-kind square Bakelite bangles. These all have multilayered laminated corners and various treatments along the sides including laminated stripes, confetti dots, and larger polka dots. The bangle in the foreground has a checkerboard liner, and is one of the best of this type. These are very difficult and laborious to make, and only a few exist. 5/8" wide up to 1-1/4"+ wide, each. $1,000+ each. Barbara Wood.

A one-of-a-kind square Bakelite bangle, with multilayered laminates on the corners, and confetti dots along the sides. 3/4" wide+, each. Ron and Ester Shultz.

A one-of-a-kind square Bakelite bangle, with multilayered laminates on the corners, and along the sides. 1/2"+ wide. Ron and Ester Shultz.

A one-of-a-kind, especially chunky, squared Bakelite bangle. Formed over a multicolored checkerboard liner, with intricately laminated corners that have been bevelled at the edges. 7/8" wide, with varying wall widths up to an astonishing 11/16" at the corners. $900-1000. Lori Kizer.

Octagons & Checkerboard Lined Bangles

Loosely derived from checkerboards, the Shultzes have made a few octagon-shaped bangles that are composed of very long, narrow checkers, some of which are overlaid on checkerboard liners. Others feature wide wedges of narrow checkers. Some have checkerboard centers, with contrasting checkerboard edges. By making the checkerboard the liner of a bangle, such as on some of the square bangles above, the Shultzes have taken the checkerboard motif even further. A few of these are then overlaid with dots or ovals. All of these types of Shultz bangles are very desirable because so few of them exist.

An unusual octagonal Bakelite bangle, formed over a multicolored checkerboard liner with striped lamination on four sides of the outside. 1/2" wide up to 5/8"+ wall at the corners. $1200. Barbara Wood.

An octagon-shaped bangle with multicolored checkerboard borders flanking a rare clear blue violet checkered center. 3/4" wide, with varying wall widths from 3/8" to 7/16". $800-900. Lori Kizer.

An unusual octagonal Bakelite bangle. The interior liner is formed from oversized Bakelite checks, and there is lamination on four sides of the outside. Transparent ruby red and green with laminated sides in aqua, yellow, and purples. 1/2" wide. $1,000. Barbara Wood.

On the bottom, an unusual octagonal Bakelite bangle with a checkerboard liner and laminations on the outside. 1/2" wide. $1000. On the top, a multicolored three-layer checkerboard octagon. 7/8" wide. $1,500. Barbara Wood.

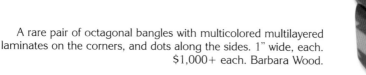

A rare pair of octagonal bangles with multicolored multilayered laminates on the corners, and dots along the sides. 1" wide, each. $1,000+ each. Barbara Wood.

Special Checkerboards

On a precious very few checkerboard bangles, the checkerboards are overlaid with dots or ovals, or chunks of the checkerboard alternate with areas of plain Bakelite. On these bangles, the checkerboard is the background instead of the focal point of the bangle. These are rare and desirable. The Shultzes have made a very few bangles on which Belle ovals are micro-checkerboarded, with many very tiny pieces. Because of their intricacy, they merit being placed in this category as well. On the ultimate Shultz checkerboards (shown last) the checkers themselves are composed of intricate laminates featuring especially hard-to-execute curved laminates. Although collectors especially prize all of these special checkerboards, checkerboards in this category are the best of the best.

A very special checkerboard. Two rows of yellow and blue Bakelite, overlaid with black fingernails and red dots. 1" wide, 3/8" wall. $1100-1250 Private collection.

A pair of Bakelite two-row checkerboard bangles which are further embellished with Belle ovals. On the right, a one-of-a-kind transparent green and frost, overlaid with four double "Belle" ovals with black on the top and transparent underneath. 7/8" wide, 5/16" walls. $950-1150. Helene Lyons. On the left, a lemon and lime two-row checkerboard overlaid with six periwinkle blue Belle ovals. 1" wide, 3/8" walls. $850-950 Karima Parry.

An unusual one-of-a-kind black and white Bakelite checkerboard bangle overlaid with large black "Belle" ovals. 1" x 3/8" walls. $900. Barbara Wood.

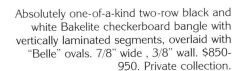

Absolutely one-of-a-kind two-row black and white Bakelite checkerboard bangle with vertically laminated segments, overlaid with "Belle" ovals. 7/8" wide , 3/8" wall. $850-950. Private collection.

A very special older Bakelite bangle. Two rows of yellow and creamed corn checkers are separated by a thin laminated layer of creamed spinach, and the whole design is overlaid with small multicolored pastel confetti dots. 1-1/2" wide, 1/4" walls. $1,500. Barbara Wood.

A similar piece, made later than the previous one in a slightly different size. Two rows of checkers are separated by a thin laminated layer, and accented with plain borders and overlaid with small confetti dots. 1-1/4" wide, 3/8" walls. $1,200. Barbara Wood.

A possibly one-of-a-kind black and transparent green Bakelite three-row checkerboard bracelet with clear vertically laminated insets which have yellow dots. 1-3/4" wide, 3/8" wall. $1000-1150. Private collection.

On the top, a very-few-of-a-kind bangle made from oversized transparent red and translucent yellow Bakelite checkers in the middle row, with black and applejuice checker borders. The "bulging" silhouette of this bangle is especially interesting and unusual. 1-1/4" wide, 3/8+ walls. $1250. Karima Parry. On the bottom, a black and applejuice two-row checkerboard bangle, overlaid with red fingernails. Private Collection.

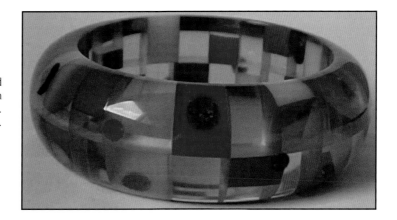

Definitely one-of-a-kind multicolored opaque and transparent Bakelite checkerboard bangle, with polka dots scattered overall. 1" wide, 1/2" walls. $2,000. Barbara Wood.

A very special one-of-a-kind red, clear and yellow Bakelite two-row checkerboard bangle. The red checks are inlaid with curved slices. 1" wide, 3/8" walls. $1800+. Barbara Wood.

A very special one-of-a-kind red, chalk green, yellow, and clear Bakelite, two-row checkerboard bangle. The colored checks are inlaid with curved slices. 1-1/16" wide, 5/8". $2,000+. Barbara Wood.

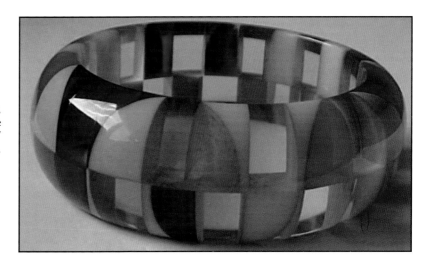

Dovetails

Also known as "Indian" bangles by some Shultz collectors because their design appears to resemble American Indian motifs, dovetail bangles are some of the most intricately laminated Shultz bangles in existence. They are rare, and valuable. Arguably, they are the best of the best, and few Shultz collectors will ever own one, as they exist in very small quantities.

A one-of-a-kind Bakelite dovetail bangle. Dovetails in green and ivory alternate with multicolored stripes, constructed over a red liner, with black borders. 1-1/4" wide, 5/16"+ walls. $1,000+. Barbara Wood.

A classic burgundy and ivory Bakelite "Indian" bracelet, constructed over a burgundy liner. These bangles are so named because the series of dovetail-laminates placed between the borders looks like an America Indian motif. The Shultzes have made very few "Indian" bracelets, and they are highly coveted by collectors. 1-7/8" wide, 1/4" wall. $1100-1300+. Private collection.

Deep wine and white Bakelite dovetail bangle on black with black borders. Note how the darker borders change the total look of the bangle. 1-1/2" wide, almost 1/2" walls. $1800-2000. Barbara Wood.

Constructed over a green liner, a green and white Bakelite dovetail-laminated "Indian" bangle. 1-1/4" wide, 3/8" walls. $1000+ Barbara Wood.

A very rare red and white Bakelite dovetail-laminated "Indian" bracelet with red borders, constructed over a red liner. 1-7/8" wide, 1/4" wall. $2000. Barbara Wood.

A chunky-walled light yellow and green Bakelite dovetail-laminated "Indian" bangle, constructed over a green liner. 1-7/8" wide, 7/16" wall. $1400+. Barbara Wood.

A green and white Bakelite dovetail-laminated "Indian" bracelet, with butterscotch borders, constructed over a contrasting liner. 1-1/2" wide, 3/8" wall. Ron and Ester Shultz.

An unusual bordered Bakelite bangle alternating red and white dovetail-laminates with black checks. Ron and Ester Shultz.

Combination Dovetails

A few bangles exist which combine dovetails with other design techniques including ribs, dotting, checkerboard-bordered, dovetail bangles, and dovetailed dots.

A pair of one-of-a-kind very detailed dovetail-laminated Bakelite bangles with checkerboard borders, constructed over liners. 1" wide, 3/8"+ walls, each. $1500-1800, each. Barbara Wood.

Red Bakelite bangle, with large "Belle" ovals, which are overlaid with dovetail-laminates. 7/8" wide, 3/8" walls. $350. Lori Kizer.

Very unusual Bakelite bangle. The middle layer has alternating checkers and dovetail-laminates. The border is confetti-dotted. Ron and Ester Shultz.

A matched set of three Bakelite bangles. The center bangle is ivory with large double "Belle" ovals of burgundy-over-black. The side bangles have alternating dovetail-laminates and chunks, constructed over a black liner. The entire set is 1-5/8" wide, and has 3/8" walls. $2000-2500. Kathleen Baker..

A matched pair of green Bakelite bangles, which are overlaid with green and white Bakelite Dovetails alternating with groups of multicolored chunks. Each measures 7/16" wide, 3/8" walls. $1000-1200 for the pair. Lori Kizer.

Reverse Carving

Ester has often told me that reverse carving is time consuming and challenging. She wrote: "My earliest reverse carves were all fish. I was so nervous about doing them. Some of them were pretty primitive but I hope that I have gotten better with practice. I think the next thing was the bee jar pins.

I also did some Lucite pins with the beach scenes. I didn't start doing flowers until a few years ago. Then I progressed to trying other things but still haven't done a lot of variety. I am always aware of the fact that when I start cutting into the bracelet, all I have to do is slip or dig too deep and then I will spoil a beautiful Lucite or Bakelite bracelet."

And those Bakelite bracelets can be expensive. A nicely proportioned vintage transparent Bakelite bangle that is suitable for reverse carving can cost well over $100. And they are becoming scarce as collectors snap them up.

Ester continued, "Even today I have to be especially motivated to go out and reverse carve. If I am feeling that it is not carving day, then it just won't work. If it is a good day and I am relaxed and have my heart in it, then I can do whatever I want to."

Ester is not overly fond of painting in the reverse-carved bangles. She confided, "The hardest thing for me in all of this is the painting. I want every thing to be perfect and spend most of my time cleaning the paint off and starting over. That generally takes hours!"

One of the author's favorite Shultz pieces is a slightly marbled Applejuice Star Dust Bakelite bangle that Ester reverse-carved and painted with a large alligator. He is a one-of-a-kind. Another fortunate collector has his cousin, a one-of-a-kind reverse-carved Lucite bangle that features a lizard.

A stack of three reverse-carved Bakelite bangles. From the bottom, an early reverse-carved fish bangle, 3/4" wide, 3/8" walls, $750-850. Kathleen Baker. In the center, a later reverse-carved and painted fish bangle 1" wide, 3/8" walls, $850-950. On top, a vaseline reverse-carved and painted bees and flowers bangle, 15/16" wide, 5/16" walls, $675-750. Both, Karima Parry.

A reverse-carved and painted Lucite "bees in a jar" pin, with laminated Bakelite lid. $400. Karima Parry.

A very special one-of-a-kind marbled Stardust Bakelite bangle, reverse-carved and painted with a large alligator and cattails. 1" wide, 5/16" walls. $2000+. Private collection.

One-of-a-kind reverse-carved and painted Lucite iguana lizard bangle with cattails. 1" wide, 3/8" walls. $800-950. Marcia Rybak.

Reverse Carving Without Painting

The earliest reverse-carved Shultz bangles feature fish and other sea life. Reverse carving was mainly done on Applejuice Bakelite bangles, but the Shultzes also did reverse carving on Lucite bangles.

One-of-a-kind chartreuse green Bakelite reverse-carved "Crocodile" pattern bangle. This bracelet is one of its owner's absolute favorites. 1-1/4" wide, 1/4" walls. $800-900 Marcia Rybak.

Two Lucite reverse-carved fish bangles. Note that the fish are swimming in opposite directions. Ron and Ester Shultz.

Reverse Carving With Painting

Most of the later reverse-carved Shultz bangles are painted . Subjects include fish and sea life (lobsters, starfish, and seahorses are especially rare and desirable), flowers, birds, scenes, and multi colored dots.

One-of-a-kind Stardust Bakelite reverse-carved and painted black-eyed Susan bangle. The black-eyed Susan pattern is not one-of-a-kind, however that it is done on a Stardust blank makes this a very special piece. 3/4" wide, 5/16" walls. $1000+. Karima Parry.

The following are four reverse-carved and painted fish bangles. The first is a transparent green Prystal Bakelite bangle with reverse-carved and painted fish. 1" wide, 5/16" walls. $600. Barbara Wood.

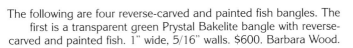

On a four-sided Lucite bangle, reverse-carved and painted fish and seaweed. $425-525. Barbara Wood.

An octagon-shaped Lucite bangle, reverse-carved and painted with fish and seaweed. $425-525. Barbara Wood.

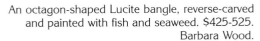

A Lucite bangle, reverse-carved and painted with fish and seaweed. 1" wide. $425. Barbara Wood.

Lucite reverse-carved and painted bees and flowers clamper bracelet. Same pattern on both sides. 3/4" wide, 3/8" walls. $500-600. Marcia Rybak.

A stack of three reverse-carved and painted Lucite clamper bracelets. The Shultzes do very few clamper bracelets. Private collection.

A wide chunky transparent lavender Bakelite bangle, reverse-carved and painted with a scene including palm trees and coconuts. 1-1/4" wide, 3/8" walls. Ron and Ester Shultz.

A wide applejuice Bakelite bangle, reverse-carved and painted with hummingbirds and flowers. 1-3/8" wide, 5/16" walls. Ron and Ester Shultz.

Lucite reverse-carved and painted dots bangle. Ester says that she did not carve the ridges on this bracelet. However, because she used a pre-carved blank, (something she very rarely does) this piece is likely one-of-a-kind. 3/4" wide, 3/8" walls. $400-500. Marcia Rybak.

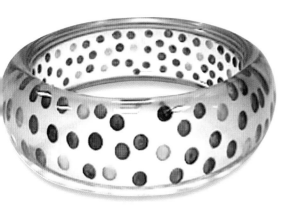

A transparent, unusual ice blue Bakelite bangle, reverse-carved and painted with multicolored dots. 1" wide, 3/8" walls. $850-900. Karima Parry.

Two reverse-carved and painted dot bangles. The wider one appears on the cover of this book. It is a one-of-a-kind, on chartreuse applejuice Stardust Bakelite, with multicolored dots, 1-1/8" wide, 5/16" walls. $1000+. Karima Parry. The narrower one is peachjuice, with red and black dots, 3/4" wide, 3/8" walls. $750-850, Kathleen Baker.

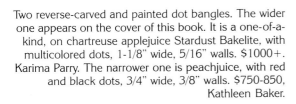

Unusual Shultz Pieces

Certain items are unusual to find in Shultz Bakelite jewelry. Necklaces and earrings are prime examples. The Shultzes have made very few of them, so any that exist are very rare indeed. Ester commented, "There aren't many necklaces out there. They take lots of time and lots of materials to make. Just putting that chain together is a major ordeal." Rings are another item that exist in strictly limited quantities. Sets featuring a matching ring and bracelet are not common, as are cuff bracelets and hinged "clamper"-type bangles. Among the rarest and most expensive of Shultz bangles are those on which a carved figural such as a parrot is repeated all around the bangle.

One-of-a-kind alligator carved Bakelite bangle. Fully carved Shultz bangles are quite rare, and this one has very heavy and detailed carving, along with applied black rhinestone eyes. He also appears in *Bakelite Bangles Price and Identification Guide*. $2,000+ Barbara Wood.

A Bakelite and Lucite cherry necklace with (especially rare) matching earrings. On a celluloid chain, the cherries are Bakelite, the opaque green leaves are plastic, and the transparent green leaves are Lucite. Ron and Ester Shultz.

A rare early necklace features seven orange marbled Bakelite oranges, three cherry vanilla marbled Bakelite cherries, and three lemon marbled Bakelite lemons, which are each accented with a pair of transparent green hard plastic leaves. All are suspended from a double linked red celluloid chain. Total length: 26". $300-450. Helene Lyons.

This early necklace features six pairs of yellow carved Bakelite bananas interspersed with seven cherry vanilla marbled Bakelite cherries, which are each accented with a pair of transparent green hard plastic leaves. All are suspended from a double-linked navy celluloid chain. Total length: 26". $300-450. Helene Lyons.

A group of four early, one-of-a-kind Shultz Bakelite rings. The Shultzes have not made many rings, so all of them are scarce. From the left: a toffee marbled ring shank with large caramel button laminated on the top. $100-150; a light green marbled and dark green laminated plaque set diagonally on top of a gold and coffee irregularly shaped shank. $125-175; a yellow marbled and red marbled laminated plaque set on top of a green marbled shank. $125-175; and a silver mercury US dime set on top of a black ring shank. $150-200. All pieces Helene Lyons.

Matched ring and bracelet sets are rare. This one is made in black and white Bakelite, with the bangle alternating wraparound dots and "Belle" ovals. The matching ring has black confetti dots. $500, the set. Private Collection.

A matched ring and bracelet set in red and black Bakelite. The bangle has "Belle" ovals all around. The matching ring has huge domed dot. $450, the set. Private Collection.

A rare matched ring and bracelet set. This one features a square bangle in red, white, and blue Bakelite, with laminated corners. The matching ring repeats the motif along the top of the ring. $550 ,the set. Private Collection.

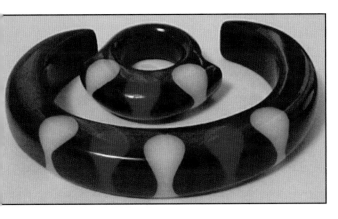

The best matched ring and bracelet set! Yellow and red Bakelite "injected dot" bowties, on a cuff, and a matching ring. $1150, the set. Private Collection.

This matched bracelet and ring set may have taken its design inspiration from the famous "Philadelphia" bracelet. Black Bakelite, with two opposing rows of multicolored, protruding laminated fins. The matching ring repeats the design, with fewer fins. $650 the set. Private Collection.

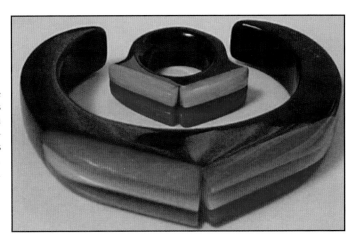

A very rare set of three carved Bakelite cuff bangles, each with a figural design: a fish, a seahorse, and a Scottie. Ron and Ester Shultz.

A rarer creamed corn "clamper" hinged-type Bakelite bangle, (the Shultzes have made very few clampers) featuring a beautifully carved and laminated bird. $600-800. Chuck Piantieri.

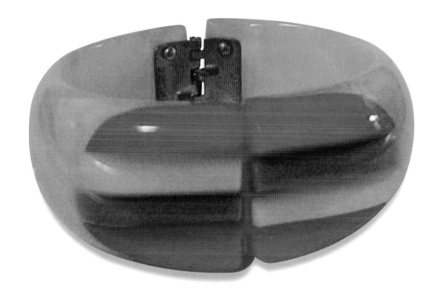

This clamper-type bangle may have its design inspiration from the famous "Philadelphia" bracelet. Two multicolored horizontally laminated elements top each half of the bracelet, and meet at the middle to form the completed design. $1800+. Private Collection.

A rare clamper-type bangle, this one is black and green Bakelite with checkerboard panels on top of each end of the bracelet. $1100+. Private collection.

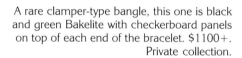

One-of-a-kind "open" checker bangle in yellow, red and creamed spinach Bakelite. This very unusual bracelet appears in *Bakelite Bangles Price and Identification Guide*. 1-1/2" wide, 3/8" walls. $1,000. Barbara Wood.

A matched one-of-a-kind pair of pink and green Bakelite bangles with inlaid Bakelite flowers and leaves in different colors. 1-1/8" wide, 3/8" walls, each. Pink, $750. Barbara Wood. Green, private collection.

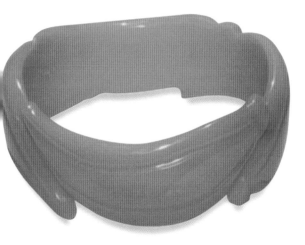

A one-of-a-kind Bakelite carved figural banana bangle. $1500. Jenaay Brown.

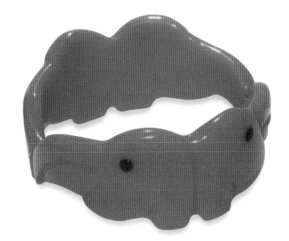

A one of a very few pink Bakelite carved flamingo heads figural bangle, with laminated eyes. $1000. Jenaay Brown.

A rare and special carved figural green Bakelite bangle with fish all around with glass eyes. Ron and Ester Shultz.

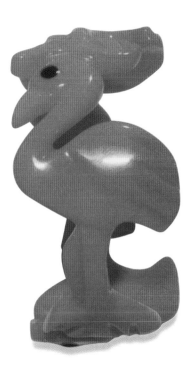

A one-of-a-kind carved figural pink flamingo Bakelite bangle, with laminated black eyes. $1500. Jenaay Brown.

One-of-a-kind carved fish bangle in black Bakelite with laminated yellow accents and applied eyes. Widest point is 1-1/2". $1,500+. Barbara Wood.

A one-of-a-kind carved Bakelite figural parrot bangle, in rare turquoise Bakelite with glass eyes and applied laminated wings. Private collection.

An especially rare carved figural Bakelite bangle with a fish on one side, and a laminated palm tree on the other. Ron and Ester Shultz.

The reverse of the fish and palm tree bangle. Ron and Ester Shultz.

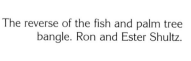

Prototypes or "Compulsive" Pieces

Ron Shultz loves to experiment. Sometimes he'll sit down at his bench to work and something amazing, absolutely experimental, and utterly unrepeatable will result. Ron and Ester refer to these pieces as "Compulsive Art," and these are the ultimate prizes for any Shultz collector. Three of the four pieces shown here have an almost architectural approach to the appearance of the ovals laminated on top of the bangles. Instead of floating on top, as the ovals usually appear, the ovals on these bangles appear to sit on top of supporting Bakelite columns.

An unusual, extra chunky, one-of-a-kind ice blue Bakelite bangle, laminated in vertical sections with pastel marbled Bakelite, and then overlaid with four HUGE purple "Belle" ovals. 13/16" wide, 1/2" walls. $1000+. Private collection.

A one-of-a-kind, extra chunky trio of transparent Bakelite bangles, each with vertically laminated slivers between the transparent panels. One with pink, one with iris purple, and one with yellow. Private Collection.

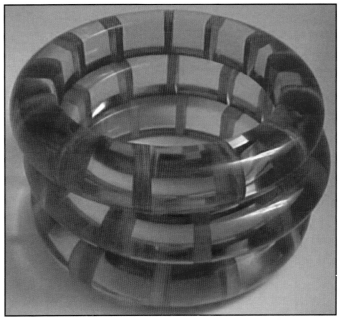

A unique one-of-a-kind "compulsive art" Bakelite bangle created by Ron Shultz. Transparent Bakelite with two purple "cat's eye" dots, and two purple vertically laminated "legs" that appear to hold up a huge purple "Belle" oval. 1/2" wide, 3/8" walls. $1000+. Karima Parry.

Companion to the piece on the left, a unique one-of-a-kind experimental "compulsive art" Bakelite bangle created by Ron Shultz. On a transparent Bakelite bangle are two purple "cat's eye" dots in different sizes and in different shades of purple, which are inlaid into the bangle. Two "Belle" ovals float along the top, one in pink, and one in purple, with a laminated purple column appearing to hold up the purple oval. It is doubtful that there will ever be another piece like either of these, as Ron confided that he cannot quite remember exactly how he accomplished the "cat's eye" dots! This bangle and its companion are the author's all time favorites. 1/2" wide, 3/8" walls. $1000+. Karima Parry.

Shultz Pins

A group of four pins, including a Scottie chained to his doghouse, a pair of carrots, a high-heeled oxford shoe, and a lobster with applied antennae. These pins range from $350-475, each. Ron and Ester Shultz.

The following pin styles are commonly found in vintage Bakelite pins, and the Shultzes have utilized them in their own pieces as well: jointed figures; bar pins with hanging items either dangling from brass loops or from celluloid chains; and pins with various items attached to them with plastic covered cord. Pin designs that are characteristically vintage but have been reinterpreted by the Shultzes would include: Scottie dogs, hats, horses, hands, fruit and vegetables. In all cases, the Shultzes have been meticulous to avoid copying old designs. Although they do sometimes make renditions of traditional motifs and designs, their pieces vary from the vintage ones that inspired them in terms of the colors used, sizes, subtle design variations, etc. Most importantly, the Shultzes sign their work with an engraved signature to identify their pieces and to prevent anyone from ever attempting to pass them off as vintage.

Valuing Shultz pins can be especially difficult. In general, the same criteria used for bangles should be applied. However, with pins, extra value should also be given to a piece that incorporates especially laborious multiple techniques, such as a pin which is carved, laminated, reverse-carved, and painted, for example.

Many Shultz pins appeared in my book, Bakelite Pins, and I felt that it would be redundant to include those same pins in detail again in this book Therefore, the pins shown and described in this chapter are all pins which did not appear in Bakelite Pins. On the back cover of this book is a collection of photos of groups of Shultz pins from Ron and Ester Shultz's own scrapbook. Some of these pins do appear in more detail in this book, while others appear in Bakelite Pins, and others we were unable to locate. I am including these group photos anyway so that you can see as many Shultz pins in this book as possible.

Red and black Bakelite shoe pin. Private collection.

Not for the timid! An overscaled black Bakelite heart pin with lots of Bakelite thingies suspended from black celluloid. 4-1/2" x 3". $500. Barbara Wood.

Red Bakelite bar pin, with black and red loops suspended from a red celluloid chain. 2-3/4" x 3". $450. Barbara Wood.

An early bright cherry red carved Bakelite heart pin, with laminated black key. 2-1/2" x 2-1/2". $375-500. Helene Lyons.

Red Bakelite key with a hanging puffy heart. 2-3/4" x 3-1/4". $800. Barbara Wood.

A red and white vertically laminated Bakelite bar pin, with suspended heart. Private collection.

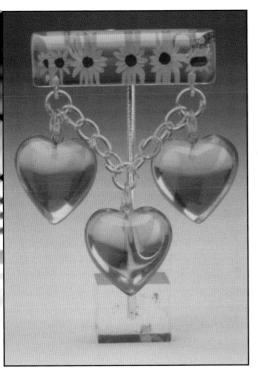

A one-of-a-kind reverse-carved and painted Bakelite bar pin with sunflowers, and three Lucite hearts suspended from a celluloid chain. $650+. Karima Parry.

An early cherry vanilla marbled Bakelite bar pin, with clear celluloid chain and six suspended cherry vanilla marbled Bakelite hearts. 3-1/2" x 3-3/4". $375-550. Helene Lyons.

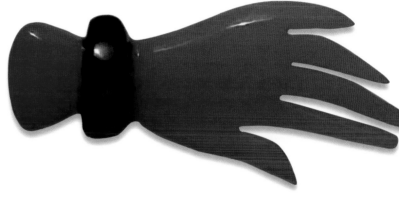

Red Bakelite hand with a Bakelite bangle (of course!) that is black with yellow dots. 3-7/8" x 1-3/4". $450. Barbara Wood.

Laminated Bakelite bar, with heart dangles suspended from celluloid chain. Barbara Wood.

Red Bakelite hand pin, with a polka dot Bakelite bangle. Private Collection.

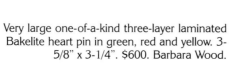

Very large one-of-a-kind three-layer laminated Bakelite heart pin in green, red and yellow. 3-5/8" x 3-1/4". $600. Barbara Wood.

One-of-a-kind four-layer laminated checker-board laminated heart pin in blue, yellow, black, and red. 2- 5/8" x 2-1/2". $800+. Barbara Wood.

Two rare Bakelite tic-tac-toe pins. Very intricately laminated, the larger is red and yellow laminated with black X's and O's. 2-3/4" across. $900. The smaller is yellow and black with red X's and O's. 1-7/8" across. $750. Barbara Wood.

Green and yellow checkerboard Bakelite hat pin, with applied cord decoration. Barbara Wood.

Transparent checked Bakelite hat pin. 2-1/2" across. $500. Jane Clarke.

A pair of black and white Bakelite checker-board hat pins with little black and white Scottie dog dangles. 2-1/2". $500, each. Jane Clarke.

One-of-a-kind Bakelite sailboat pin with laminated and applejuice sails and a blue-moon boat. 2-3/4" x 2-1/2". $500. Barbara Wood.

One of only two, a red, black, yellow and applejuice laminated Bakelite pins, with reverse-carved fish and seaweed. $450. Barbara Wood.

Very rare pale transparent blue Bakelite circle with a multi-techniques Miami scene. 2-1/2" across. $350+ Barbara Wood.

A very rare heavy carved and wonderful Indian pin in ivory, applejuice, and black Bakelite. Only two of these exist. 2-3/4" x 2-1/4". $1,000. Barbara Wood.

Red Bakelite bar pin, with four large cookie buttons and two large Bakelite balls suspended from a red celluloid chain. 4-1/4" x 4". $420. Barbara Wood.

Bakelite school pin with pencil bar, and ABC cubes, ruler, ink bottle, apple, and slate suspended from a hanging celluloid chain. 3" x 3". $550. Barbara Wood.

Astonishing Bakelite lady wearing a bead necklace and hat composed of Bakelite buttons. Private collection.

Older Bakelite school charm pin. Ruler bar, with apple, inkspot, and other charms suspended from a hanging celluloid chain. 3" x 3-1/2". $800 +. Jane Clarke.

Red Bakelite apple, with laminated stem, with carved leaf. Private collection.

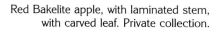

An early red Bakelite apple pin, with laminated carved applejuice leaf, laminated stem, and subtle lamination around "bite". 2-7/8" x 2". $255-375. Helene Lyons.

Pair of Bakelite carrots pin, with plastic-covered cord stems. 3-1/2" x 1-1/4". $300. Barbara Wood.

An early yellow Bakelite banana pin, with painted detail. 2-3/4" x 1-1/2". $195-300. Helene Lyons.

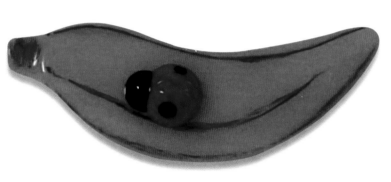

Bakelite banana pin, with painted detail, and laminated red and black ladybug. Private collection.

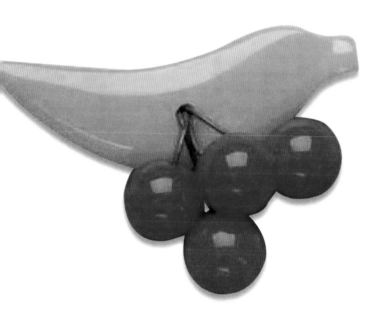

Large Bakelite banana, with four cherries suspended from plastic covered cord. Private collection.

Large green Bakelite banana leaf, with three bananas suspended from plastic covered cord. Private collection.

123

Reverse-carved Lucite bar pin, with transparent cherries and leaves suspended from a transparent celluloid chain. Private collection.

Carved Bakelite bar pin with faceted Bakelite oranges and plastic leaves suspended from chain. 3-1/2" x 3-1/4". $425. Barbara Wood.

Laminated and carved Bakelite pumpkin on a bed of leaves pin. Private collection.

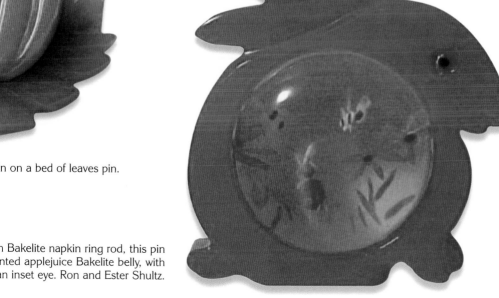

Constructed from a rabbit pattern Bakelite napkin ring rod, this pin has a reverse-carved and painted applejuice Bakelite belly, with carved detailing and an inset eye. Ron and Ester Shultz.

Constructed from a fish pattern Bakelite napkin ring rod, this pin has a reverse-carved and painted applejuice Bakelite fish bowl in its belly, with carved detailing and an inset eye. Ron and Ester Shultz.

A reverse-carved and painted applejuice Bakelite fishbowl pin, with goldfish and seaweed, and a laminated black Bakelite rim. $600. Karima Parry.

Black Bakelite bar with a large, heavy, applejuice reversed carved and painted fish bowl with painted fish and seaweed. 2-3/4" x 2-1/2. $800. Barbara Wood.

Constructed from a chicken pattern Bakelite napkin ring rod, this pin has a reverse-carved and painted applejuice Bakelite belly, with carved detailing and an inset eye. Ron and Ester Shultz.

Unusual checker Bakelite laminated bar with a laminated applejuice panel pin with reverse-carved and painted bees and flowers. Private collection.

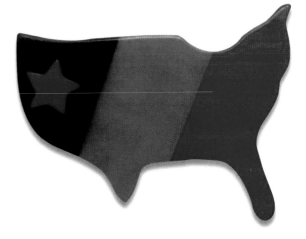

The Shultzes made a limited number of red, white, and blue patriotic commemorative pieces in the wake of the events of 9/11/01. This is a laminated Bakelite map of the United States, with inset laminated star. Judith Black Gale.

Commemorative 9/11/01, red, white, and blue laminated Bakelite map of the United States, with inset laminated heart. Judith Black Gale.

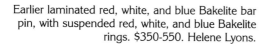

Earlier laminated red, white, and blue Bakelite bar pin, with suspended red, white, and blue Bakelite rings. $350-550. Helene Lyons.

Very special laminated Uncle Sam hat in red, white (ivory) and blue Bakelite. Signed "Shultz #1". 3" x 2-3/4". $500. Barbara Wood.

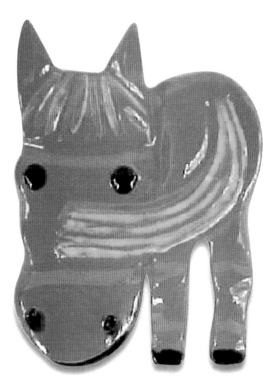

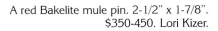
A red Bakelite mule pin. 2-1/2" x 1-7/8". $350-450. Lori Kizer.

An early, one-of-a-kind red Bakelite race horse head pin, with brass bridle studs and a glass eye. 3-3/4" x 2". $225-350. Helene Lyons.

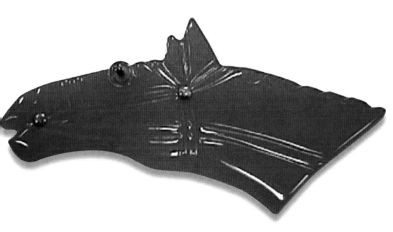

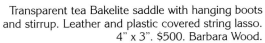
Transparent tea Bakelite saddle with hanging boots and stirrup. Leather and plastic covered string lasso. 4" x 3". $500. Barbara Wood.

An early yellow Bakelite romping French poodle pin with an inlaid black eye. 3" x 2-3/4". $255-350. Helene Lyons.

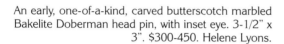

An early, one-of-a-kind, carved butterscotch marbled Bakelite Doberman head pin, with inset eye. 3-1/2" x 3". $300-450. Helene Lyons.

An early one-of-a-kind cherry red Bakelite bar pin with three suspended carved Bakelite monkeys — "speak no evil, hear no evil, see no evil" — with painted details. 2-3/4" x 3-1/2". $350-550. Helene Lyons.

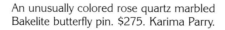

An unusually colored rose quartz marbled Bakelite butterfly pin. $275. Karima Parry.

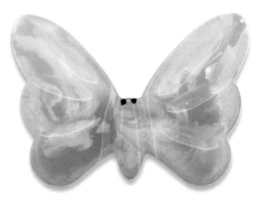

The Shultzes have made a number of limited edition Christmas tree pins. Made in 1993, an early, rarer Bakelite Christmas tree pin, with laminated star and tree trunk, and inlaid dots. $350-450 Chuck Piantiere.

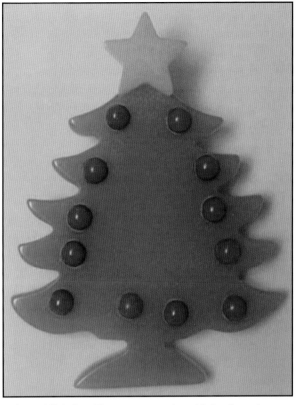

Carved Bakelite Christmas tree pin, with laminated ornaments, and yellow star on top. Note that although this is similar to the previous pin, this one does not have a laminated base. Private collection.

Unusual articulated Bakelite Christmas tree pin, with dangling bead ornaments and laminated yellow star. Kathleen Baker.

Carved Bakelite Christmas tree, with bead garlands and laminated yellow star on top. Private collection.

Red and cream Bakelite laminated Christmas tree pin with star on top. Private collection.

Laminated Bakelite Christmas tree pin with star on top. Private collection.

Red, yellow, and green checkerboard Bakelite Christmas tree pin, with a red star on top. Private collection.

Red, yellow, and green checkerboard Bakelite Christmas tree pin, with a yellow star on top, and a green laminated base. Private collection.

Unusual diagonally laminated Bakelite Christmas tree pin, with laminated yellow star on top. Private collection.

Multicolored Bakelite laminated chunks Christmas tree pin. Private collection.

A pair of Bakelite snowman pins, with painted details, bows, and black hats. Private collection.

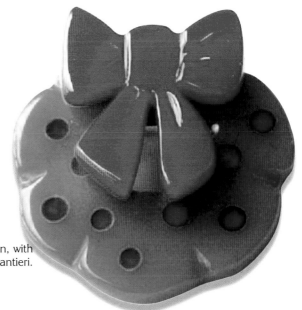

Made in 1993, a rarer Bakelite Christmas wreath pin, with laminated bow and inlaid dots. $350-450 Chuck Piantieri.

A laminated Bakelite candy cane pin, with applied carved bow. This piece was made in 1993. $350-400 Chuck Piantiere.

A pair of unusual Bakelite portrait pins. Carved with painted details. 2-1/4" x 1-1/8", each. $300 each. Barbara Wood.

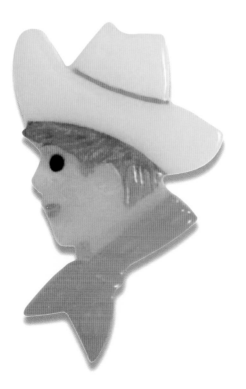

Jointed Bakelite sailor pin, 1-3/4" x 3-1/4". $400-500. Lori Kizer.

Laminated yellow, butterscotch, and red Bakelite cowboy pin with carving. Painted mouth and stripe on hat, inset eye. 3-1/2" x 2-1/2". $600. Barbara Wood.

A rare figural Bakelite lady pin. Private collection.

A similar articulated Bakelite man pin, with a wooden hat, large bow and stretchy legs. Eyes are inset. 4-1/4" x 2-1/2". $500. Barbara Wood.

An articulated Bakelite scarecrow pin, with laminated and painted details. Private collection.

Articulated Bakelite man pin, with laminated pants, "hair," and inset eyes. 4" x 2-1/2". $500. Barbara Wood.

A rare Bakelite rabbit gone fishing pin. Private collection.

An early pair of figures, constructed from pieces of Bakelite with laminated details. Articulated. Ron and Ester Shultz.

A Bakelite giraffe in front of a coconut tree pin. Private collection.

A Bakelite bear with balloons pin. Private collection.

A rare Bakelite ow jumping over the moon pin. 'rivate collection.

A carved Bakelite macaw pin, with contrasting beak and eye. Private collection.

A wonderful green and yellow intricately laminated and carved Bakelite parrot pin, with contrasting laminated beak. Ron and Ester Shultz.

An early, possibly one-of-a-kind, carved ivory Bakelite swan pin with laminated wing, inset eye, and painted detail. 3" x 2-1/2". $400-500. Helene Lyons.

Yellow Bakelite pelican pin, with red carved wing and head. Black inset eye. 3-3/4" x 1-1/2". $450. Barbara Wood.

Older yellow Bakelite chicken pin with inlaid dot eye and painted details. 3" x 3". $350. Barbara Wood.

A Bakelite penguin pin, with cream belly and laminated beak and eye. $300-400. Chuck Piantiere.

A rare multicolored Bakelite bird pin suspended on chains from a laminated applejuice and black bar pin, which is reverse-carved with flowers. $800. Barbara Wood.

An overscaled and heavy black, red, orange, green, white, blue and brown Bakelite pelican pin, laminated over a yellow base. 4-3/4" x 3". Only two of these were ever made. $600. Barbara Wood.

Extra large Bakelite flamingo pin with laminated black beak and glass eye. 4" x 2-1/2". $500. Barbara Wood.

A carved red Bakelite sailfish pin with a black inset eye. 3-1/2" x 3-1/4". $550. Barbara Wood.

A huge, early, one-of-a-kind laminated butterscotch-over-orange Bakelite marbled shark pin with inset eye. 2-1/2" x 6". $550. Helene Lyons.

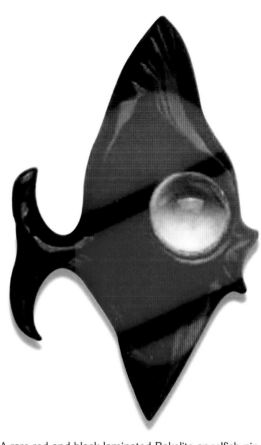

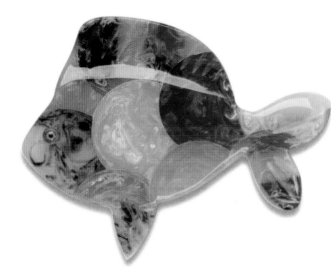

A one-of-a-kind Bakelite fish pin, covered with oversized marbled overlapping scales. Ron and Ester Shultz.

A rare red and black laminated Bakelite angelfish pin. Private collection.

Heavily carved with applied antennae red Bakelite lobster pin. 3-1/2" x 2-3/4". $425. Barbara Wood.

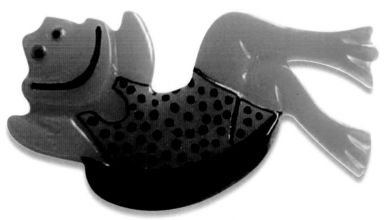

A whimsical green Bakelite frog lounging in her swimsuit on an innertube pin. $425. Barbara Wood.

An early, one-of-a-kind red Bakelite crab pin, with painted detail and painted plastic coated string eyes. 3" x 2-1/2". $300-450. Helene Lyons.

A red Bakelite lizard pin, with a black laminated stripe from head to tail. Private collection.

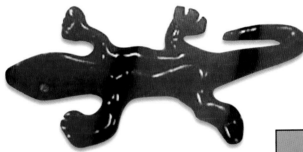

A very early unsigned (but authenticated) cherry red and black laminated Bakelite carved lizard pin, with inset rhinestone eyes. 3" x 1-1/2". $195-325. Helene Lyons.

A one-of-a-kind black and ivory checkered Bakelite lizard pin with bulging Bakelite eyes. 5-1/4" long, 2" tall. $450. Barbara Wood.

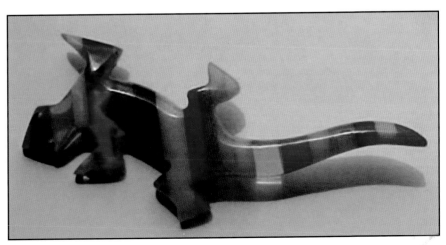

A one-of-a-kind striped lizard pin in many laminated colors of opaque and transparent Bakelite. 5-1/8" long, 2" tall. $450. Barbara Wood.

A green Bakelite alligator pin with a laminated eye. Private collection.

Likely one-of-a-kind articulated green Bakelite alligator pin hooked together with a gold chain. Very heavy carving, applied glass eye. Both the head and the tail have pinbacks. 5" long , 1-1/4" tall. $550. Barbara Wood.

Likely a one-of-a-kind, especially realistic green Bakelite lizard pin. Marcia Rybak.

A very special chameleon lizard pin. The chameleon is pink laminated on top of yellow Bakelite , and has a glass eye. It is sitting on a carved green Bakelite leaf. There is a story about how this pin came to be made. One day, Ester visited a pet store and became enchanted with a chameleon lizard she saw there. Ester is an animal lover and the Shultzes have a number of pets. She considered buying the chameleon, but knew nothing about the care of such a pet. So she e-mailed the collector who now owns this pin because she is a nationally known authority on lizards. The collector sent Ester books and addresses of web sites so that she could learn what taking care of such a pet would entail. In the end, Ester decided that she would have difficulty feeding the chameleon insects and so she did not get it. But the chameleon pin that she made instead found its way to the collector, who treasures it. 4" wide, 1-5/8" tall. $900-1000. Marcia Rybak.

The Amazing World of
Shultz Scottie Dogs

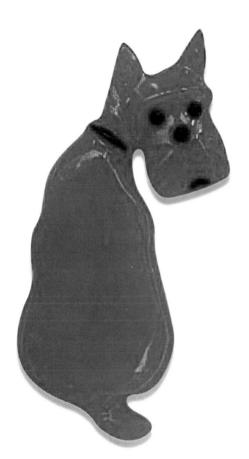

President Roosevelt had a beloved black Scottie dog named Fala, who was often photographed accompanying the President. President George W. Bush has a black Scottie named Barney. During the Roosevelt era, Bakelite jewelry designers and crafters of the day quickly realized that Fala and Scotties in general would prove to be a popular design motif for Bakelite jewelry.

Vintage Bakelite Scottie pins abound, but it was not until the Shultzes started making Scottie pins that Bakelite Scotties embarked on a whole new life. Shultz Scotties do things that vintage Scotties rarely did. Shultz Scotties wear all kinds of fantastic collars, and have been known to smoke a pipe. They have been seen wearing hats and going fishing. Some of them come complete with their own doghouse, and others only go out with friends. They march, they dance, the peer over their shoulders, and they strut around with attitude! Sydney Bohnlein and her husband, David, are longtime collectors of all kinds of antique and modern Scotties, as well as Bakelite Scotties, both vintage and Shultz. Many of the Shultz Scotties below are from Sydney's collection.

Ester Shultz has told me that she has not kept many pieces for herself. This one-of-a-kind Scottie pin, however, is one of her personal favorites. Priceless. Ron and Ester Shultz.

An overscaled carved Bakelite Scottie head pin, with laminated eye and beaded collar. Private collection.

An early cherry red carved Bakelite Scottie head pin, with glass eye and painted nose. 2-3/4" x 2-3/4". $375-475. Helene Lyons.

Intricately carved black Bakelite Scottie head, with painted eye detail. 2-1/2" across x 2-3/4" tall. $350-400. Sydney Bohnlein.

Creamed corn Bakelite side view Scottie carved head pin with black Bakelite eye and painted nose. 2-5/8" tall x 2-1/2" across. $200-225. Sydney Bohnlein.

Overscaled carved red Bakelite Scottie head pin, with laminated eyes. Private collection.

Creme Bakelite carved Scottie head pin, with glass eyes, black painted nose, and red tongue. 3-1/4" tall, 1-3/4" across. $300-350. Sydney Bohnlein.

Huge, red Bakelite Scottie head pin, with carved detail, laminated black eye, painted nose, and laminated black and yellow collar. 3-3/4" across x 3-1/2" tall. $450-525. Sydney Bohnlein.

Bright yellow Bakelite full-bodied, side-view Scottie pin with painted eye, nose and mouth. Slightly concave with exceptional carved "hair" detail. 2-5/8" tall x 2-3/4" across. $350-400. Sydney Bohnlein.

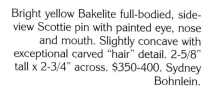

Creamed corn Bakelite Scottie romping puppy pin, with laminated black Bakelite eyes and nose, and painted mouth. 2-7/8" tall x 2-1/4" across. $350-400. Sydney Bohnlein.

Older creme Bakelite Scottie pin, with an oversized head. The head is a separate piece glued to the body. Originally a trembler, it was glued to prevent repeated repairs. Painted detail. 2-3/4" tall x 2-1/2" across. $300-350. Sydney Bohnlein.

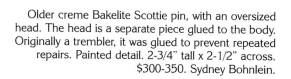

Butterscotch Bakelite Scottie pin, with carved details, black Bakelite eye and painted mouth and collar. 3-1/2" across x 3" tall. $325. Barbara Wood.

Red Bakelite seated Scottie with bow, black Bakelite eye. 3-1/4" tall x 3" across, 1/4" thick. $275-325. Sydney Bohnlein.

Butterscotch Bakelite Scottie pin with glass eye, painted nose, tongue and collar detail. 2-1/2" tall x 3-1/4" across. $350. Sydney Bohnlein.

An early bright yellow Bakelite carved Scottie pin with laminated marbled green and black checkerboard collar and eye. 2" x 2". $285-400 Helene Lyons.

Creamed corn Bakelite Scottie dog pin with laminated red bow and black eye, and painted nose and mouth. 3" across x 2-1/2" tall. $300 Barbara Wood.

Cream Bakelite Scottie pin, with laminated red bow and eye, and painted nose and mouth. Private collection.

Butterscotch Bakelite Scottie pin, with laminated red bow and black eye, and painted nose and mouth. Private collection.

Early red Bakelite kissing Scottie trembler pin with very detailed carving. Scottie ears are attached with two small springs. 1-1/4" tall x 2" across. $400-450. Sydney Bohnlein.

146

Yellow Bakelite jelly belly Scottie pin with glass eye and painted black nose. The jelly belly is reverse-carved and painted with two Scotties playing with a red ball under a couple of trees. 2-7/8" wide x 2-1/2" tall. $375-400. Marcia Rybak.

A one-of-a-kind Bakelite Scottie with fire hydrant pin. $300+ Barbara Wood.

Black Bakelite Scottie dog, with green collar and red dog house with laminated black roof. 2" across x 2-1/2" tall. $475. Barbara Wood.

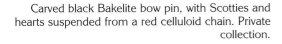

Carved black Bakelite bow pin, with Scotties and hearts suspended from a red celluloid chain. Private collection.

Butterscotch Bakelite doghouse, with laminated red roof, and with two black Scotties and a dog bone dangles. Private collection.

Red Bakelite Scottie going fishing pin with black painted shoes, hat and nose. Black Bakelite eye, yellow Bakelite fishing rod and fish. Metal fishhook, black string fish line. 3" tall x 2" across, 1/4" thick. $375-400. Sydney Bohnlein.

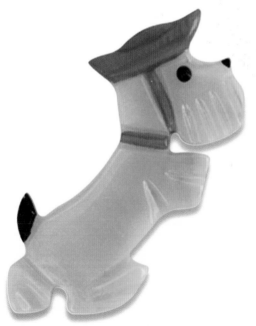

Creamed corn Bakelite Scottie sailor pin with laminated black eye, and painted hat, nose and tail. 2-3/4" tall x 3" across. $325-350. Sydney Bohnlein.

Light blue marbleized Bakelite clamper bangle with flattened ends and laminated carved black Scottie heads. $400-475. Sydney Bohnlein.

Red Bakelite hinged bracelet with flattened edges and carved laminated Scotties. $600. Sydney Bohnlein.

Rare domed red Bakelite cuff bracelet with carved Scottie head, glass eye. 2-7/8" wide, exterior dimension. $400-450. Sydney Bohnlein.

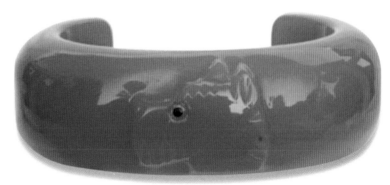

Exceptionally thick butterscotch Bakelite cuff bracelet was Shultz "Scottified" by being cut back to leave a Scottie standing in relief. Exceptional carving! Originally 1/2" thick in center of cuff. Exterior width is 3". $500-600. Sydney Bohnlein.

Chunky black Bakelite bracelet with carved Scottie heads and red laminated dots. 1-1/8" wide, 3/8" walls. $600-750. Sydney Bohnlein.

One-of-a-kind transparent red Bakelite bangle with reverse-carved Scottie heads. 1" wide, 3/8" walls. $650-700. Sydney Bohnlein.

A one-of-a-kind Bakelite bangle featuring two Scottie heads with glass eyes facing each other, and the letter "S" for "Sydney or Scottie," 1-1/2" wide, 3/8"+ walls. Cherished by the collector who owns it. Priceless. Sydney Bohnlein.

A chunky black Bakelite bangle, with carved Scottie heads with glass eyes. Private collection.

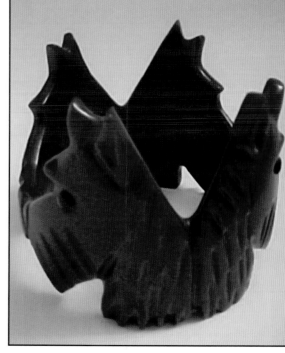

A one-of-a-kind Bakelite Scottie bangle in a rare purple with carved Scottie heads repeating four times. At widest point, measures 2-1/4". $1,500. Barbara Wood.

Collecting Shultz Bakelite

For many years, it was not necessarily easy for collectors to get their hands on Shultz Bakelite jewelry. Either they had to buy it from the Shultzes directly at one of the few antiques shows where they would set up and sell their work. Or, it had to be bought from the small circle of dealers who have been Shultz loyalists from the very beginning, and through whom the Shultzes have sold their work in the past and continue to do so. These dealers include: Barbara Wood at www.bwoodantique.com; Helene "Nini" Lyons at Remembrances of Things Past at shop@thingspast.com; Lori Kizer at www.rhinestoneairplane.com; and a very few others. Shultz Bakelite can occasionally be found on the Internet in auction venues such as e-bay, and, as original owners resell their pieces from time to time, a few pieces can be found reentering the market on websites and at antiques shows and auctions. The author also always has a selection of Shultz Bakelite on her own website at www.plasticfantastic.com . In general, Shultz collectors become quite attached to their Shultz pieces, and have a hard time giving them up, so you won't find many reentering the market from collections!

Three unusual Bakelite bangles. From the left, a chunky pink marbled bangle with large wraparound dots that are composed of horizontally laminated multicolored slivers. 3/4" wide, 3/8" walls. $700-850. Private collection. In the center, a likely one-of-a-kind bordered checker with a clear checker bulging center, and a pink and white marbled checkered border on one side, and a mauve and white marbled checkered border on the other side. This bangle was a gift to the author from Ester Shultz, and she has a great sentimental attachment to it. 3/4" wide, 3/8" walls. Priceless. On the right, a pink marbled bangle encircled with multicolored fingernail dots with squared bottoms set on their sides, and polka dots. This is probably a one-of-a-kind piece. 7/8" wide, 5/16" walls. $650-850. Karima Parry.

Wearing Shultz Bakelite

As the author discovered when she acquired her first Shultz bangle, Shultz Bakelite is happiest when worn with other Shultz Bakelite. Shultz does marry well with transparent vintage pieces, and the occasional opaque or translucent piece, but, on the whole, combining Shultz pieces with vintage Bakelite jewelry can create an uneasy match, with the intense vivid colors of the Shultz pieces making the vintage pieces look aged, dark, and even unappealing by comparison. For the devoted Shultz collector who has accumulated a number of Shultz pieces, combining them into pleasing groups to wear is a delicious pursuit. Below are a few examples of bangle stacks put together from pieces in the author's collection, and from the collections of other ardent Shultz collectors. Even Ron and Ester can be surprised at the combinations that their collectors manage to come up with!

A pair of Shultz Bangles in different techniques and complimentary colors creates a dramatic statement. In this stack, a chunky domed red bangle with two rows of black fingernail dots pairs with an overscaled wraparound dotted bangle. Barbara Wood.

A three piece "go together" set of Bakelite bangles. In the center, a three-row laminate of white marble with shocking pink on the edges, then overlaid with six large purple marbled wraparound dots. On either side, a matched pair of purple marbled flying saucer bangles, with long pink Belle ovals. Private collection.

A very special stack of four Bakelite bangles, featuring rare colors. From the bottom, an extra chunky applejuice and purple two-row checkerboard. 1" wide, 7/16" walls, $800-950. Next, a unique experimental transparent Bakelite bangle with two purple "cat's eye" dots, and two purple vertically laminated "legs" that appear to hold up a huge purple Belle oval. 1/2" wide, 3/8" walls. $1000+. Then, a rare one-of-a-kind purple Bakelite two-row checkerboard bangle. Opaque fuchsia purple squares alternate with very rare translucent purple, lilac, and creme marbled squares. 7/8" wide, 3/8" walls. $1000+. Finally, at the top, a very special one-of-a-kind Stardust applejuice Bakelite bangle, with four large rare purple ovals floating along the surface. 1" wide, 5/16" walls. $1000+. All, Karima Parry.

Matched pairs of narrow bangles are especially useful when creating stacks. In this stack of three Shultz Bakelite bangles, a matched pair of narrow bangles with wraparound dots flank a square Bakelite bangle in complimentary colors with laminated corners and dotted sides. Private collection.

A matched pair of narrow wraparound dotted Bakelite bangles, flank a single green Bakelite bangle with two rows of black fingernail dots.

A stack of various techniques, black and white Bakelite bangles. Barbara Wood.

A stack of five burgundy-moon marbled Bakelite bangles. Two matched pairs, one with black six dots and the other with aqua marbled "Belle" ovals. 1/2" wide, 3/8" walls, each. $800, per pair. Karima Parry. In the center, a single bangle with double "Belle" ovals in green and fuchsia, over white. 1/2" wide, 3/8" walls. $750. Private collection.

A stack of seven blue-moon marbled Bakelite bangles. Two with wraparound dots, four with "Belle" ovals, and one with double "Belle" ovals. Bangles range from 1/2" to 3/4" wide, all have 3/8" walls. $450-750, each. Karima Parry.

A stack of three Bakelite bangles in complimentary colors and varying techniques. On the bottom, a black and applejuice checker-bordered cherry juice and lemon checker with an uncommon bulging center silhouette. 1" wide, 1/2" walls. $1200+. In the center, a narrow cherry juice with black "Belle" ovals. 1/2" wide, 5/16" walls. $375. On top, a cherry juice and opaque lemon two-row checkerboard. 7/8" wide, 3/8" walls. $800. Karima Parry.

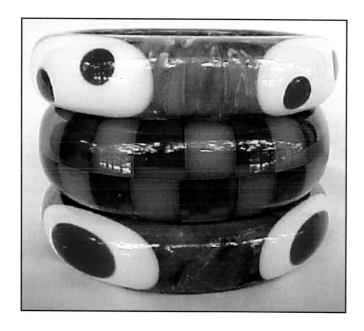

A Bakelite "go together" matched set. In the center, a two-row checkerboard. Above, a bangle with dotted "Belle" ovals. On the bottom, double "Belle" ovals. Lori Kizer.

A stack of four Bakelite bangles, in varying techniques. On the bottom, red with yellow "Belle" ovals. Next one up is black, with yellow and red confetti dots. Third from the bottom is a black, red, and yellow two-row checkerboard. On top, a red with yellow marbled confetti dots. Karima Parry.

A stack of three Bakelite bangles including two square bangles with laminated corners and dotted sides. The one on the top has rarer dovetailed corners. In between, a green and red two-row checkerboard bangle. Private collection.

154

Shultz Bakelite Collectors

Barbara Wood

Helene (Nini) Lyons

Barbara Wood, and her friend Happy.

Helene (Nini) Lyons.

I started collecting Ester and Ron Shultz Bakelite jewelry about 9 years ago. I met Ester and Ron in Florida and fell in love with them along with their wonderful art made from old Bakelite pieces salvaged from broken radios, jukeboxes, etc. All of their pieces are individual pieces of art and no two are absolutely identical. I prefer to wear stacks of 3 to 5 bangles in different sizes. I have a favorite combination of black and Applejuice checks with Applejuice and black dots that I like to wear all the time. I also have a fabulous Applejuice with black Bakelite parrot pin and a large unusual carved bird pin. One of my all time favorites is a wonderful one-of-a-kind carved alligator bangle that is very special. I also have an Indian pin that is a favorite.

I was fortunate enough to meet Ron and Ester Shultz, the Bakelite magicians, in the '80s on a field in their spot under a tree in Brimfield, Massachusetts. The sight of their work started a smile that has broadened during the years of knowing them and their incredible work. Not only are they true artists, they're grand human beings! Their art brings such delight to the eyes of the beholder, collector, and wearer! I'm proud to know them as friends and artists.

Lori Kizer

Sally Loeb

Lori Kizer.

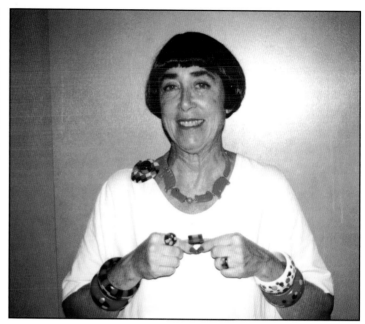

Sally Loeb.

We had seen and admired Shultz items for a few years before buying any. There was always a concern about authenticity and value as a collectible. We finally purchased on of their specialties, a "random dot" bangle. A little later, we bought a plain bangle and sent it to Ester to have dots added. Both bracelets are beautiful. We especially admired the Shultz items that did NOT closely resemble or "copy" the Bakelite items made in the 1930s-1950s. We loved their original designs. That's how and why we purchased additional items: bracelets, pins, rings and a necklace. We love them all!

I've been collecting Shultz for, I guess, 8 years now. My first Shultz piece was a soldier dog pin. Even though I rarely wear pins any more they remain among my favorites. I enjoy just having them around to look at as miniature pieces of art. Same thing with their bangles. I'm always amazed to see what new designs Ron and Ester's fertile imaginations come up with. As raw Bakelite material gets scarcer, their inventiveness and skill at using even tiny pieces seems boundless.

Marcia Rybak

A triple row black and applejuice Bakelite checkerboard bangle. 1-3/8" wide, 3/8 " walls. $850-950. Lizard and bangle, Marcia Rybak.

Bonnie Robinson Wallace

Bonnie Robinson Wallace.

I keep and breed lizards and turtles so I am naturally attracted to jewelry with a reptilian theme. I first became really interested in Bakelite while shopping looking for lizard jewelry. I liked the old Bakelite pins and started expanding my searches to include all the Bakelite jewelry. That is when I first discovered Shultz Bakelite jewelry. Shultz pieces are among the very few Bakelite bracelets and pins identified with a designer name and I was intrigued. Once I saw that first piece of Shultz I was hooked. Shultz jewelry is the best of both worlds. It combines the old material and look with innovative designs and a contemporary finish. I have several one-of-a-kind pieces created by Ester, which include an alligator, two lizard pins and probably my favorite piece, a reverse-carved "croc" bangle.

I have been collecting Ron and Ester's Bakelite bangle beauties for about a year. Of course, Shultz is an addiction like any other, and once you start, you can't stop. My first Shultz set that I wore in public was to the March , 2001 Pier 88 show in New York City. I was strutting around in Bakelite heaven with a particularly striking pair of lemon, red, and black fingernails and another bangle with wraparound dots, and I stopped to talk with a lovely dealer who had a small, albeit, wonderful collection of vintage carveds and laminates. As I was looking at only "vintage" Bakelite, she said to me, "But you're wearing 'new' and they are so beautiful." And I said to her, "Of course they are. They're SHULTZ!" Her eyes widened and she grinned as if to say "Wow"! It was a leveling of the playing field of sorts. "New" was no longer necessarily bad.

Randy Isaacson

Sydney Bohnlein

Randy Isaacson.

I believe my first romantic encounter with my beloved Bakelite occurred when I was approximately 6 years old, as I stood quietly by my Mother while she was playing Mah Jong and listening to the clacking sound of the Bakelite tiles and reaching out to fondle them during game clean-up. The smoothness, the coolness as well as the warmness, and the sound the tiles made as they rapped together were a sensual experience for me. I knew I wanted to be around it as part of my life's pleasures, even at that young age.

In 2000, I began seeking out Bakelite on the Internet and came across a three-row red and yellow checked bangle bracelet described by the seller as made by "Shultz." I had heart palpitations immediately, and purchased it online as fast as my fingers could type the keys! When I received this gorgeous piece of red and yellow checked splendor, it became my favorite and most adored piece of jewelry. I wore it every day, with every color of clothing—even if it didn't match! It just made me feel simply happy! I knew I had to find more, and thanks to the Internet I soon did, and my collection continues to grow and grow.

I am a collector of Scottie dog memorabilia, especially Scottie jewelry.

In 1992, my sister Amy returned home from the Brimfield, Massachusetts, antique extravaganza talking about the wonderful Bakelite Scotties she had found. Later that same year, while antiquing with my husband, David, at the Carlisle, Pennsylvania antique show, we accidentally found those wonderful pieces in a booth. In the rear of that booth we met Ron and Ester Shultz.

It has been my pleasure over the years to introduce other Scottie collectors to the Shultzes' work at our annual convention of Scottie collectors, and I am looking forward to another decade of collecting Shultz Scottie pieces. Thank you Ron & Ester.

Kathleen Baker

Karima Parry

Kathleen Baker.

Karima Parry.

Bakelite jewelry means a lot to me. It makes me feel good inside. It wasn't until four years ago that I began to hear the name Shultz being associated with Bakelite jewelry. Over and over again I heard the name, yet no one was able to point me in the right direction to find it. Feeling a little frustrated, at a 1997 costume jewelry convention, I had the surprise of my life. At last, I came upon a large collection of Shultz Bakelite. I was amazed by the beauty, design, style, and workmanship, and there were many of those large "statement" pieces that I especially like. The ones that make people say "WOW" when they see them. Well need I say I was hooked? You bet.

My collection of Shultz has increased dramatically since I "discovered" it. There is no doubt in my mind that as contemporary jewelry designers their passion is reflected in all of their work. Ron and Ester Shultz are making a mark in jewelry design history.

Shultz Bakelite grows on you. That first piece is an awakening; colors you never realized or expected existed in Bakelite, designs that are tantalizing and graphically exciting, and meticulous craftsmanship. The next piece you acquire, ostensibly to keep the first piece company, is the beginning of a journey. But Shultz Bakelite is not a private obsession. Shultz collectors wear their Shultz pieces and share them with everyone that they meet. Everywhere I go, people stop me to comment on my bangles. Their initial attraction is to the colors, but they invariably want to examine them closely, and to run their fingers over their glossy colorful surfaces. The reaction is always the same: everyone loves them. They make people smile.

In Conclusion

The world of Shultz Bakelite is a happy place, where Scotties go fishing, where you can wear your heart on your sleeve, or the contents of your refrigerator vegetable crisper on your lapel. Bright colors and vivid patterns are everywhere, and a stack of colorful Shultz bangles looks like a party on your wrist. So, how do Shultz collectors define beautiful? Arguably, for each individual, the definition is as unique as they are. The range of Shultz Bakelite pieces is sufficient that each collector can concentrate on collecting those pieces which are beautiful to them. There are Shultz collectors who collect only pins, or only bangles. Some specialize even further, such as the collector who concentrates only on Shultz Scottie pieces. But for all of us, a beautiful Shultz is the one that makes us happy, and all of them do. And Shultz collectors will tell you that Shultzes make other people happy too. Shultz Bakelite makes friends wherever it goes.